Living BY THE Light OF THE Moon

2017 Moon Book

Beatrex Quntanna

Disclaimer

Before following any Yoga advice or practice suggested by this book, it is recommended that you consult your doctor as to its suitability, especially if you suffer from any health problems or special conditions. The publishers, the author, and associates cannot accept responsibility for any injuries or damage incurred as a result of following the exercises in this book, or using any of the therapeutic methods described or mentioned.

ISBN 978-0-9625292-7-6

Printed in the United States of America

ART ALA CARTE PUBLISHING
760-944-6020
beatrex@cox.net
www.mymoonbook.com
www.beatrex.com

Acknowledgments

Master teacher and mystic Nancy Tappe—my dear friend and my mentor—inspired me and encouraged me to manifest the teachings in this book. Thank you, Nancy.

Thank you to…

- Jennifer Masters for the cover art *Victory,* and for her ability to capture the true nature of acceleration with her magical graphic art.
- Michelenne Crab for her personal support and for her tech support for the last 16 years.
- Michael Makay for the daily Tibetan numerology intentions that inspire and direct us to make the most of each day.
- Kate Thomas for taking on the job of editing my creative chaos. I appreciate your spontaneous abilities and your understanding of my knowledge as *knowing* not as academia.
- Jennifer "Tashi" Vause, RYT for *Sky Power Yoga,* taking the time to determine yoga poses for each moon. So much fun to add the physical domain to astrology!
- Katherine Sale for the astrological calculations for the entire year.
- Kaliani Devinne for contributing the goddess profiles that correspond to each moon cycle and the moon charts.
- Jill Estensen for sharing aspects from *Dimensional Astrology* that add an innovative approach to experiencing the degrees and the polarity that they create for each moon phase.
- Candice Covington for her approach to the elements.
- Ann Meyer for the freedom affirmations from *Teaching of the Inner Christ.*

Special thanks to the countless students who come to Moon Class—without you this teaching would not exist!

Production Credits

- Art Direction, Book Design, and Cover Art *Victory*—Jennifer Masters—JenniferMastersCreative.com
- Editing—Kate Thomas—LotusLama.com
- Daily Tibetan Numerology—Michael Makay—mbmakay@gmail.com
- Sabian Symbols *Dimensional Astrology*—Jill Estensen—intuvision@roadrunner.com
- Astrological Calculations—Katherine Sale, MSW, MAc—StargazerKat@gmail.com
- Goddess Profiles—Kaliani Devinne—StepsOnTheSacredSpiral.blogspot.com
- Yoga *Sky Power Yoga*—Jennifer "Tashi" Vause, RYT—yogatashi@yahoo.com

About the Art

This is my fifth year working on the *Living by the Light of the Moon Book* with Beatrex, bringing her teachings and ideas to life in visual form. Each year has been its own amazing journey of discovery and co-creation, beginning with the overarching theme she sets for the year. Working with Beatrex is truly a collaborative process, which is a blessing since the average graphic design project doesn't allow me to stretch my creative wings quite as far as this.

The Tibetan Numerology for 2017 is "10" which symbolizes the concepts of victory, celebration, goals, vision, innovation, new beginnings, and acceleration into the future—these are the themes we will all be playing with for the year.

When I was busy trying not to meditate on what should go on the cover because I was driving at the time, the name *Nike* sprang to mind—no, not the shoe! I thought to myself, oh yeah, she's like the goddess of speed or something, isn't she?

I did a little research when I got home, and discovered she would indeed be an appropriate symbol for a 10 year. Nike is the Greek Goddess of Victory, sometimes called Winged Victory. Depicted with one of her symbols, the laurel wreath, she was honored at the Olympic Games in Ancient Greece, and is still pictured on the Olympic metals awarded today. She is also "The Flying Lady" decorating the hood of every Rolls Royce automobile.

The next day, a documentary comes on while I'm watching television, all about owls and how quickly and proficiently they can swoop in and hit their intended target. Inspired by their grace and speed, I immediately knew I'd be modeling her wings after owl wings! After Beatrex wrote a statement about accelerating our knowledge beyond what we imagined possible, the owl, a symbol of knowledge, seemed all the more appropriate.

I had started out thinking I would paint Nike soaring through the cosmos in long, flowing robes. But as I pieced together a composition to show Beatrex my idea for her approval, I really fell in love with the flying lady you see here on the cover, yellow crop top, rolled-up blue jeans, et al. Beatrex said, "of course, 10 is all about updating ourselves and accelerating into the future!" Confirmation that I was definitely on the right track with the art.

Guided by the Goddess Nike, Beatrex helped me brainstorm visual ideas for acceleration, and we settled on the twelve symbols you see on the pages of the calendar.

- Mount Everest pointed skyward with prayer flags whipped up by the wind.
- Bamboo which symbolizes rapid growth.
- Rockets symbolize speeding toward our future vision, and this rocket is inspired by NASA's Orion spacecraft, currently being developed for human exploration of the planet Mars.
- The Flamenco dancer with accelerated footwork, spinning faster and faster.
- Cheetahs are the fastest land-mammal on the planet.
- In addition to The Flying Lady atop the Rolls Royce, we have more "flying" ladies—a runner, a surfer, a skateboarder, and a broom-stick rider.
- An arrow flying towards its goal, represented by archer and Goddess, Diana.

There is always more to the story, and many more layers of meaning, but feel free to draw your own conclusions—that is, after all, what art is all about!

—Jennifer Masters
Artist, Illustrator, Creative

Photo by Jean Frédéric

THIS BOOK IS DEDICATED TO

The Flying Lady

WHO GRACES THE ROLLS ROYCE—AN ELEGANT SYMBOL OF

victory through acceleration and motion.

MAY WE ALL *accelerate* THIS YEAR AND

WAVE OUR WINGS IN *victory!*

Table of Contents

The Importance of Cycles

The Moon is the keeper of the secrets of life and its cycles set the stage for successful living. Beatrex has developed a valuable collection of knowledge about how to use the cycles of the Moon to enhance the quality of your life. This workbook reveals those secrets and supports you in implementing them. Each cycle offers a different combination of light energy to give you the chance to grow harmoniously into wholeness. Following the luminaries, the Sun and the Moon, through the zodiac and noting the cycles of illumination and reflection can bring you to a deeper creative experience of life. The Moon is the great cosmic architect—the builder and the dissolver of form. Full Moons are about dissolving and New Moons are about building. This workbook will assist you in knowing what and when to build and what and when to dissolve with activities for each cycle of the Moon throughout 2017.

Life, at the highest spiritual level, moves beyond time and uses cycles to increase your ability to actualize your full potential. Cycles are in charge of your personal development; while time is in charge of the change in direction that happens when you evolve by trusting in divine timing. This workbook synthesizes techniques that allow for the power of development and direction to occur in the entire spectrum of wholeness. Each zodiac sign holds the knowledge necessary to integrate an aspect of yourself to become whole. As the Moon and the Sun travel around our planet each month, a different aspect of self-development is presented to you via the zodiac sign constellation that it visits.

The Year of Acceleration keeps our manifesting ability available to us each moment. The more we manifest—by allowing the bliss from our spiritual essence to come forward—the less we suffer. Give up being devoted to the past and embark on new frontiers. Adjust and recalibrate the core of your being. This workbook instructs you how to manifest and to recalibrate so that the power of acceleration becomes your reality in 2017.

Please note: All times listed in the book are local to the Pacific time zone. Add or subtract hours accordingly to adjust times for your time zone. It is best to do your manifesting and recalibrating ceremonies at the specific time noted. Visit www.mymoonbook.com for mirrors.

When the Moon is Full

It is time to set yourself free when the Moon is full and in direct opposition to the Sun. This polarity dissolves anything that stands in the way of your personal recalibration. Sixty hours before a full moon you may experience tension as the Sun and the Moon oppose each other. Learn to understand the opposite natures without feeling the need to separate them. Find the middle ground so that you are not manipulated by polarity as the integration of opposites creates the unity that creates harmony.

The polarity themes are on each full moon's page. Use the astrological theme to inspire you to renew your life by writing a recalibration list. Light a candle and read your list out loud. Place your recalibration list under a circle-shaped mirror and put your candle on top of the mirror. Make sure to use a candle in glass—a votive or seven-day candle—to protect from fire. Place outside in the moonlight or in a special place in your home. Let the candle burn out. When your candle is finished burning, your list is in operation. Empty space allows manifestation to occur. Before writing your list you might want to look over the full moon cycle's trigger points to see if there is anything you need to let go of first. Remember recalibration allows you to live without resistance.

When the Moon is New

When the Moon is new, it is in the same sign as the Sun. This unites the power of the magnetic and the dynamic fields that are in perfect resonance for manifesting. This is a potent time to make your desires known by writing your manifesting list. Use the astrological theme to write your list like a child who is writing to Santa Claus. Be comfortable with extending your list's boundaries beyond what you believe is possible by thinking: *This, or something better than this, comes to me in an easy and pleasurable way for the good of all concerned.* Then light a candle and read your list out loud. Place it under an eight-sided mirror and put your candle on top of the mirror. Make sure to use a candle in glass—a votive or seven-day candle—to protect from fire. Place outside in the moonlight or in a special place in your home. Let the candle burn out. By the time the candle burns out, your list is in operation.

How To Use This Book

These Sections Will Help You to Live by the Light of the Moon

Planetary Highlights

This section explains the planets and how they will affect your life each month. It does not contain all of the aspects; it simply highlights points of interest that promote personal growth during each month. If you are interested in more study, take an astrology class. If you are an astrologer and want more information, we have provided a chart for each moon phase for your convenience.

The Monthly Calendar

This section provides you with a monthly overview and keeps you connected to the lunar, solar, and planetary cycles. It lets you know when the Moon is void-of-course, when it moves into a new sign, when the Sun and planets change signs, and when a planet goes retrograde or stationary direct (shown by the $\frac{S}{D}$ symbol). The calendar also has the Tibetan Numerology of the Day, along with an affirmation, to help you align with the energy and set your intentions for the day.

Void Moon

When the Moon is void-of-course, it has made its last major aspect in a sign and stays void until it enters the next sign. When the Moon is void-of-course, you will see the icon V/C on the calendar. This is not a good time to start new projects, relationships, or to take trips, unless you intend to never follow through. When the Moon ☽ enters a new sign, you will see this arrow ➡ It will be followed by the symbol for the new sign and the time that the Moon enters it.

Super-Sensitivity ▲

This happens when the Moon travels across the sky, hits the center of the galaxy, and connects with a fixed star. When this happens the atmosphere becomes chaotic. An extra amount of energy pours down in a spiral at a very fast speed making it difficult to focus. This fragility can make you depressed, anxious, dizzy, and accident-prone. It is a good idea to keep your thought process away from this energy. This is global, not personal.

Low-Vitality ▼

This happens when the Moon is directly opposite the center of the galaxy. When this fixed-star opposition occurs, the Earth becomes very fragile and gets depleted. This leads to exhaustion in our physical bodies and is a sign for us to nurture ourselves by resting. The depletion can create Earth changes. Endings can also happen and resistance to these completions will bring on exhaustion. Best to detach and let go.

The Sun

Each month you will see the icon for the Sun ☉ with an arrow ➡ indicating when the Sun enters a new sign. When the Sun changes signs, the climate of energy takes on a new theme for your personal development. Look for the Sun icon, with an arrow followed by an astrological sign, to indicate sign change and time.

Planets

Planets also change signs and move in retrograde and direct motions. Retrograde planets are next to the date in each day's box followed by retrograde icon ℞. In the middle of each box is information about planetary changes of time and direction.

Please note: All times are given for the Pacific time zone. Add or subtract hours accordingly to adjust times for your time zone.

"I" Statements

These statements align the Self with the characteristics of the astrological sign and the house the sign lives in.

Body Mind Spirit

Each astrological sign rules a body part, a mental trait or attitude, and a spiritual condition. This section is provided to increase understanding of the tendencies and patterns that are activated during the moon transit.

Elements

Each moon cycle has a primary element (earth, air, fire or water), attached to the constellation to which it is assigned, that brings you more awareness of what to work on during the cycle.

Choice Points: Light – Shadow – Wisdom

Dimensional Astrology presents us with a prescribed action for each of the 360-degrees on the astrology wheel. The object of Dimensional Astrology is to depolarize and neutralize. Each degree for the Moon and its house are described to better enhance your understanding of the phase and its effects on you and your world. The wisdom comes when we experience and combine the motivation and the resistance without judgment. For example, in the new moon in January, the Choice Point light is about accepting praise, the shadow side is gossip. You will find yourself accepting praise, and if you resist you set yourself up for gossip. The wisdom is accepting praise and acknowledgement and in so doing others accept their own authority.

House Themes

Each house the Moon lands in brings a focus for that moon as a baseline for self-development during the moon phase.

Karmic Awakenings

Every once in a while the chart for the Moon will show an intercepted astrological sign in a house on the chart. This indicates that a karmic pattern is in operation on that day.

Goddesses

When the Moon enters a new zodiac sign, a changing of guardians occurs. Deep within each sign lives a goddess who is the keeper of this cyclical domain. This archetype's assignment is to hold the space for an aspect of wholeness to actualize.

Build Your Altar

An altar is an outer focus for inner work. Esoteric coordinates such as Tarot cards, flowers, colors, gemstones, fragrances, and numerology are provided as an enhancement to better assist you in working with each moon phase. Perhaps you are working on a love theme; you might want to add six hearts, six flowers, and six gemstones on your altar with your manifesting list and candle. The coordinating tarot card can be used as a visual activation. Flowers, colors, and gemstones accent your intentions. The fragrance provides a special connection to Spirit. You may want to burn candles of this scent, spritz your aura or your altar with the fragrance, or simply sniff the fragrance to awaken your olfactory system. *Visit www.mymoonbook.com for moon mists.*

Clearing the Slate

This is the first step to recalibrate and release during each full moon cycle. Each section is filled with trigger points that are specific to the astrological sign where the Moon resides. See if any of them feel familiar. Acknowledge what's familiar and then follow the instructions by writing down what happened and perform Ho'oponopono, the Hawaiian forgiveness ritual. For example, a negative trigger point for Leo is impatience. When you find yourself being impatient, write down the circumstances or journal about it. Then, looking in the mirror, apologize to yourself, ask for forgiveness, have gratitude for yourself with thanks that you could see your impatience as a trigger, and then return to love.

Challenges and Victories

These are sets of affirmations designed to say out loud during a specific moon cycle to determine a motivational tone for your self-discovery. After saying all of them out loud, you will know which statement applies to you. Circle the one that is yours and use it as a personal mantra daily during the moon phase.

Recalibrating List

Write down what you wish to accelerate beyond your life's current paradigm.

Activate Acceleration

Acknowledge what you have overcome during the Moon's releasing cycle to make way for acceleration to occur.

Manifesting List

Write down what you want to create and manifest in your life.

Gratitude List

Keep adding to your Gratitude List throughout the entire manifesting cycle to activate and encourage the flow of miracles in your life. Acknowledging completion makes way for new levels of opportunity to occur.

List Ideas

Use these ideas to jump start your own lists. Let your imagination take off from here.

Sky Power Yoga

After manifesting, recalibrating, facing your trigger points, and becoming open to being victorious, yoga can physically support the energy of transformation in your life.

Please consult your doctor if you need to determine whether yoga exercises are suitable for you. If a pose is contraindicated for you, energetic benefit can still be obtained by envisioning the steps rather than doing them physically. Otherwise, proceed from a modified stance that has been medically-approved for you.

Before following any advice or practice suggested by this book, it is recommended that you consult your doctor as to its suitability, especially if you suffer from any health problems or special conditions. The publishers, the author, and associates cannot accept responsibility for any injuries or damage incurred as a result of following the exercises in this book, or using any of the therapeutic methods described or mentioned.

The Astro Wheel

Western astrological charts are placed within a circle or wheel. The wheel is a picture of the sky from a particular place and time on Earth. It is divided into 12 parts called "houses." Each house deals with a particular area of life.

Key concepts for each house are written outside the wheel. Compare the wheel in the book to your very own chart and discover the theme that you will be living personally during the moon phase.

You will want to use a natal chart for yourself that clearly shows the degrees and the houses. For the preferred chart to use with this book, visit www.mymoonbook.com/moon-class and look for the link to download a free chart. You will need to know the date, time, and place of your birth.

Cosmic Check-In

"I" statements are designed specifically to keep you in touch with all of the signs and their houses each time the Moon is new or full. Fill in the blanks to complete each statement during each full and new moon phase to activate all parts of your birth chart and keep you in touch with Oneness. Have fun noticing how different you are during each cycle.

Blank Pages

Between each moon phase blank pages are provided for journaling.

Heavenly Bodies

☉	Sun	Outer personality, potential, director, the most obvious traits of the consciousness projection
☽	Moon	Emotion, feelings, memory, unconsciousness, mother's influence, ancestors, home life
☿	Mercury	The way you think, the intention beneath your thoughts, communication, academia (lower mind)
♀	Venus	Beauty, value, romantic love, sensuality, creativity, being social, fun, femininity
♂	Mars	Action, change, variety, sex drive, ambition, warrior, ego, athletics, masculinity
♃	Jupiter	Benevolent, jovial, excessive, expansive, optimistic, abundant, extravagant, accepting good fortune
♄	Saturn	Teacher, karma, disciplined, restrictive, father's influence
♅	Uranus	Liberated, revolutionary, explosive, spontaneous, breakthrough, innovation, technology
♆	Neptune	Mystical, charming, sensitive, addictive, glamorous, deceptive, illusions
♇	Pluto	Money, wealth, transformation, secrets, hidden information, sexuality, psychic power
⚷	Chiron	Wounded healer, healing, holistic therapies
☊	North Node	This represents where you are headed in this lifetime. In other words, it represents the direction your life will take you, your future focus. In Eastern astrology, this is sometimes called the "head of the dragon."
☋	South Node	This represents what you brought with you this lifetime and what you are moving away from. It is sometimes called the "tail of the dragon" in Eastern astrology.

Astrological Signs

Each sign of astrology has a particular quality or tone that is described in more detail with the moons.

Sign	"I" Statement		Element	Key Words
♈ Aries	I Am	Sign of the Ram Ruled by Mars ♂ Aries begins the zodiac year with the Spring Equinox	Fire	Ego, identity, championship, leadership, action-oriented, warrior, and self-first.
♉ Taurus	I Have	Sign of the Bull Ruled by Venus ♀	Earth	Self-value, abundant, aesthetic, business, sensuous, art, beauty, flowers, gardens, collector, and shopper.
♊ Gemini	I Communicate	Sign of the Twins Ruled by Mercury ☿	Air	Versatile, expressive, restless, travel-minded, short trips, flirt, gossip, "nose for news," and messenger.
♋ Cancer	I Feel	Sign of the Crab Ruled by the Moon ☽ Cancer begins with the Summer Solstice	Water	Emotional, nurturing, family-oriented, home, mother, cooking, security-minded, ancestors, builder of form and foundation.
♌ Leo	I Love	Sign of the Lion Ruled by the Sun ☉	Fire	Willful, dramatic, loyal, children, child-ego state, love affairs, decadent, royal, show-stopper, theatre, adored and adoring.
♍ Virgo	I Heal	Sign of the Virgin Ruled by Mercury ☿	Earth	Gives birth to Divinity, perfectionist, discernment, scientific, analytical, habitual, work-oriented, body maintenance, earth connection, attention to detail, service-oriented, earth healer, herbs, and judgmental.
♎ Libra	I Relate	Sign of the Scales Ruled by Venus ♀ Libra begins with the Autumnal Equinox	Air	Relationship, social, harmony, industry, the law, diplomacy, morality, beauty, strategist, logical, and over-active mind.
♏ Scorpio	I Transform	Sign of the Scorpion Ruled by Pluto ♀ and Mars ♂	Water	Intense, passionate, sexual, powerful, focused, controlling, deep, driven, and secretive.
♐ Sagittarius	I Seek	Sign of the Archer Ruled by Jupiter ♃	Fire	Optimistic, generous, preacher-teacher, world traveler, higher knowledge, goal-oriented, philosophy, culture, publishing, extravagance, excessive, exaggerator, and good fortune.
♑ Capricorn	I Produce	Sign of the Goat Ruled by Saturn ♄ Capricorn begins at the Winter Solstice	Earth	Ambitious, concretive, responsible, achievement, business, corporate structure, world systems, and useful.
♒ Aquarius	I Know	Sign of the Water Bearer Ruled by Uranus ♅	Air	Inventive, idealistic, utopian, rebellion, innovative, technology, community, friends, synergy, group consciousness, science, magic, trendy, and future-orientation.
♓ Pisces	I Trust	Sign of the Fishes Ruled by Neptune ♆	Water	Sensitive, creative, empathetic, theatre, addiction, escape artist, glamor, secretive, Divinely guided, healer, medicine.

The Astro Wheel

Western astrological charts are placed within a circle or wheel. The wheel is a picture of the sky from a particular place and time on Earth. It is divided into 12 parts called "houses." Each house deals with a particular area of life. Below are some key concepts for each house.

	Statement	Ruling Sign		Key Notes
1st House	**I Am**	♈	Aries	Your outer appearance, the way you present yourself, the way you dress, the way you enter a room, and what you leave behind when you leave the room.
2nd House	**I Have**	♉	Taurus	The way you make your money and the way you spend your money.
3rd House	**I Communicate**	♊	Gemini	How you get the word out and the message behind the words.
4th House	**I Feel**	♋	Cancer	The way your early environmental training was and how that set your foundation for living, and why you chose your mother.
5th House	**I Love**	♌	Leo	The way you love and how you want to be loved.
6th House	**I Heal**	♍	Virgo	The way you manage your body and its appearance.
7th House	**I Relate**	♎	Libra	One-on-one relationships, defines your people attraction, and how you work in relationships with the people you attract.
8th House	**I Transform**	♏	Scorpio	How you share money and other resources, what you keep hidden regarding sex, death, real estate, and regeneration.
9th House	**I Seek**	♐	Sagittarius	The way you approach spirituality, philosophy, journeys, higher knowledge, and aspiration.
10th House	**I Produce**	♑	Capricorn	Your approach to status, career, honor, and prestige, and why you chose your Father.
11th House	**I Know**	♒	Aquarius	Your approach to friends, social consciousness, teamwork, community service, and the future.
12th House	**I Trust**	♓	Pisces	Determines how you deal with your karma, unconscious software, and what you will experience in order to attain mastery by completing your karma. It is also about the way you connect to the Divine.

Tibetan Numerology of the Day

2	**Balance**	Be decisive and move past vacillation.
3	**Fun**	Have a party. Take on a creative project. Express the "Disneyland" side of yourself.
4	**Structure**	Take the day to organize. Get the job done. Work and you will sail through the day.
5	**Action, exercise, travel**	Exercise—join a gym, take a dance class, play tennis, go for a walk. Travel—go for a drive, travel the world, visit your travel agent. Make a change.
6	**Love**	Go out for a night of romance. Work on beauty in your home. Nurture yourself and take care of your health.
7	**Research**	Read a book. Learn something new and get smart. Take a class.
8	**Money**	Have a business meeting. Meet with your accountant. Make a sales call. Start a new business.
9	**Connecting with the Divine**	Meditate. Take part in a humanitarian project. Do community service.
10	**Seeing the "big picture"**	Take an innovative idea and run with it today!
11	**Completion**	Do what it takes to be complete.

January

Planetary Highlights

Until January 8: Mercury retrograde in Capricorn

The new year begins with a single retrograde left over from 2016. This creates a bit of a delay—a backlash—from *The Year of Generosity*. Mercury, the ruler of thinking, is retrograde in Capricorn. Did you forget to learn anything last year? Do you need to update anything to advance with gusto into *The Year of Acceleration*? This seven-day grace period allows us to recalibrate our thoughts so we don't waste time in 2017.

January 8: Mercury direct in Sagittarius

Let's go! The mind moves from the practical, slow-moving earth element of Capricorn into the adventurous, fast-moving fire element of Sagittarius.

January 8-9: Super Sensitivity

The erratic atmosphere creates a seesaw of expansion and contraction. Avoid personalizing any communications and research what is up and what is down. Understand each influence and add your positive intentions to both sides of the energetic equation.

January 10-11: Low Vitality

Nurture yourself. The earth needs energy and could zap you if you don't take care of yourself. Drink water, get rest, and revitalize your body in gentle ways.

January 10-12: Pluto and Sun in Capricorn

What are your powers? Add intention to the powerful aspects of yourself so that your year can soar far beyond your wildest dreams.

January 12: Jupiter opposite Uranus

Throughout 2017, life's outer expression is distorted as both planets' expansion fields are vast and unconventional. Ideally this creates acceleration via enthusiasm, but watch out if your enthusiasm clouds your better judgment. Don't forget the practical side of life. This expansive field can lead to dissatisfaction and restlessness with norms and traditions.

January 12-15: Saturn and Mercury coupled in Sagittarius

To avoid dualistic thinking take on a research project.

January 12-16: Venus and Neptune dance in Pisces

Expect your rose-colored glasses to be working overtime in fantastic ways! Enjoy a wild ride to the outer realms of wonder knowing that fantasy is good as long as you don't get intoxicated by the illusion.

January 12-16: Mars conjunct Chiron in Pisces

Focus on the wounded side of your masculine self. Where didn't you stand up for yourself? Man up to rectify and recalibrate your masculine energies.

January 24-25: Super Sensitivity

The erratic atmosphere creates a seesaw of expansion and contraction. Avoid personalizing any communications.

January 27: Lunar New Year—New Moon in Aquarius

The lunar new year of the fire rooster begins at 4:07 PM, bringing the dawn of new awakenings, triumph, and success. Success and good fortune are achieved through hard work and taking action towards your goals. The lunar year's yin fire element is magnetic and will increase your inner wisdom, insights, and intuition. Connect with family and friends to enjoy the heart-warming energy of the fire rooster.

SUNDAY	MONDAY	TUESDAY	WEDNESDAY	THURSDAY	FRIDAY	SATURDAY
1 ♀℞ New Year's Day ☽V/C 11:58PM 3. Create from your heart's desire.	**2** ♀℞ ☽→♓ 1:57AM ♀→♓ 11:48PM 4. Be logical in your dealings today.	**3** ♀℞ 5. Change gives you the ability to grow.	**4** ♀℞ ☽V/C 8:14AM ☽→♈ 8:19 AM ♀℞→♐ 6:18AM 6. Make your home a sacred space.	**5** ♀℞ 7. Know what is right for you.	**6** ♀℞ ☽V/C10:41AM ☽→♉ 12:17 PM 8. Generosity keeps abundance alive.	**7** ♀℞ ☽V/C 6:22PM 9. Pray with a loving heart.
8 ▲ ☽→♊ 2:06 PM ♑-28°♐51'-1:44AM 10. Celebrate a new beginning.	**9** ▲ 2. Stay in balance and all will be fine.	**10** ▼ ☽V/C 1:38PM ☽→♋ 2:48 PM 3. Playing refreshes the spirit.	**11** ▼ 4. Look at both sides of the issue.	**12** ○22°♋27'3:33AM ☽V/C 3:33AM ☽→♌ 4:07 PM ♀→♑ 6:04 AM 5. Adapt to change and be free.	**13** 6. Flowers make you feel loved.	**14** ☽V/C 7:16AM ☽→♍ 7:52 PM 7. Learn something new today.
15 8. Be a leader without followers.	**16** Martin Luther King ☽V/C 10:09PM 9. Love for humanity requires action.	**17** ☽→♎ 3:15 AM 10. Move on and drop the past.	**18** 2. Gather the facts, then decide.	**19** ☽V/C 12:54AM ☽→♏ 2:09 PM ○→♒ 1:25PM 3. Let experience guide your truth.	**20** 4. Team players play together.	**21** ☽V/C 5:24PM 5. Remember variety is the spice of life.
22 ☽→♐2:45 PM 6. Support your friends in loving ways.	**23** 7. Resting the mind is beneficial.	**24** ▲ ☽V/C 9:33AM ☽→♑ 2:43 PM 8. Good leaders are good listeners.	**25** ▲ 9. Pray out loud, it works better.	**26** ☽V/C 11:17PM 10. Reliving the past is pointless.	**27** Lunar New Year ●8°♒15'4:07PM ☽→♒12:36 AM ♂→♈ 9:40 PM 2. Once you decide, don't look back.	**28** ☽V/C 9:52PM 3. Find joy in all you do.
29 ☽→♓ 8:10 AM 4. A good foundation gives good support.	**30** 5. Choose to move in a new direction.	**31** ☽V/C 9:35AM ☽→♈ 1:46 PM 6. Let your soul respond to music.				

Full Moon in Cancer

January 12th, 3:33 AM

Statement I Feel
Body Breasts
Mind Security
Spirit Building Form
Element Water – Sensitive, creative, empathetic, theatrical, glamorous, secretive, divinely guided, the addict, the escape artist, and the healer.

Degree Choice Points
22° Cancer 26'
Light Discussion
Shadow Disinformation
Wisdom See beyond beliefs, rationalizations, and expressions of subjective reality.

Twelfth House Moon
6° Cancer 57'

Eighth House Umbrella Theme
I Feel /I Transform - How you share money and other resources, what you keep hidden regarding sex, death, real estate, and regeneration.
Light Healing Imagination
Shadow Too good to be true
Wisdom All experience is valuable for evolution.

The Sun is Opposite the Moon

Full moons are always in opposition to the Sun. This creates a feeling of tension between where you want to shine and how your feelings are flowing on a sensory level about the Sun's directive. The two forces seem like they are working against each other, yet they are on the same team displaying different techniques to obtain the same mission. The Cancer/Capricorn polarity creates tension between being at home with your family or being at work positioning yourself for success.

Cancer Goddess

Birds are the symbol of expanded consciousness because they are born twice; once into the egg and once out of the egg. They are associated with rebirth and self-realization. Bird Woman is the Cancer goddess. She teaches us that, although we live in the illusion that security comes from our identity in the outer world, our true cosmic significance must be found within. Bird Woman directs us toward discovering our way home to our Soul, the place of lotus light. She has the ability to fly between Heaven and Earth, bringing communications from the angels and the spirit guides. She inspires souls to infuse matter with light—the true essence of co-creating.

Build Your Altar

Colors Shades of gray and milky, creamy colors
Numerology 5 – Go for variety, power, and expansion
Tarot Card The Chariot – The ability to move forward
Gemstones Pearl, moonstone, ruby
Plant remedy Shooting Star – The ability to move straight ahead
Fragrance Peppermint – The essence of the Great Mother

Clearing the Slate

Sixty hours before the full moon, negative traits connected to the astro-sign might become activated to trigger what needs to be released during the full moon phase. You may notice an unusual amount of worry, moodiness, addiction to the past, or challenges related to the energy of mothering.

Make a list of the triggers and do Ho'oponopono, a Hawaiian Huna ritual for forgiveness. Look in the mirror, and for each negative trait, tell yourself *I am sorry, I forgive you, thank you for your awareness,* and *I love you.*

Cancer Victories & Challenges

Say all of the statements in this section out loud. Then, underline the phrase that means the most to you. Use the phrase as your special affirmation for recalibrating throughout this phase of the moon.

Today, I take advantage of my ability to take action and position myself for success. I clearly know that the road to success is before me, and all I need to do is move forward. I am aware that when I take action and move forward, the Universe fills in the dots. Whether I move left, right, or straight ahead doesn't matter—what matters is that I am in movement. Today, I release indecisiveness that keeps me stuck. Today, I let go of vacillation that exhausts my mind. Today, I take my foot off of the brakes and find the gas pedal. I allow movement to occur, even if I don't know where I am going. When I take action, I trust the guideposts will appear. I am aware that action leads me to my new direction. Today, I know and GO! I remember that Karma comes to the space of non-action, while success comes through action. Action brings me to my victory.

Standing still leads to regret, resentment, and chaos. I am aware that action can be as simple as taking a walk on the beach, buying fresh flowers to add a new dimension to my home, or simply going to a new restaurant for lunch. I take action today to break up a crystallized pattern and, in so doing, my life begins to show me newfound awareness and light to guide me.

Cancer Homework

It's now time to conquer pride and ambition, overcome fear of loneliness, release the need for money, security, and possessions, discover the value of emotions, and connect to beauty. Submerge yourself in a tub of water, relax, and let the clean water flow through your cells to wash away all of your hurts, resentments, and history that keep you trapped in the past. Pull the plug and let the spiral of water carry away your pain. Be prepared to boldly claim your presence in the present. Look around your kitchen and throw away the pots and pans that continue to feed your past, rather than vitalizing your life now.

Recalibrating List

Say this statement out loud three times before writing your recalibrating list:

I am a free spiritual being and it is my desire to be free to think and to express myself fully — to move about my life toward Truth and Wisdom — to accept and enjoy all good which is mine in living my truth.

I am now free and ready to make choices beyond survival!

Cancer Recalibrating Ideas

Now is the time to set myself free from self-pity, defensive behavior, nurturing everyone else but me, living in the past, being a mother, and having a mother.

Activate Acceleration

By acknowledging what you have recalibrated and overcome, you activate your acceleration. Keep this list active during this moon cycle.

Sky Power Yoga

Seated Cat/Cow

You need one chair for the prop.

With your back straight sit one hand-width from the back of the chair with your feet on the floor hip-width apart. If your feet require more solid contact with the floor, place pillows or folded towels under your feet.

Sit comfortably with a straight back and gently cup knees. Breathe in and out slowly and deeply several times through your nose with your awareness on your breasts.

Inhale and allow your belly to drop down as your pelvis tilts back into a subtle back bend.

As you inhale, say or think to yourself the mantra *I Feel*.

Exhale slowly as you tilt your pelvis forward and round your back slightly into a gentle forward bend while gazing down. Repeat with a smooth, continuous movement as many times as desired.

Full Moon in Cancer

How to Use the Moon Book With Your Chart

Fill in the blanks on the Cosmic Check-In page. Then look up the degree of the Moon on the chart below. Take note of the "I" statement on the outside of the wheel where the Moon is located. Now, locate the same degree on your own chart and make a note of the house and corresponding "I" statement. Go back to the Cosmic Check-In page and circle the two statements from the charts and read what you wrote. This will give you an idea about what to expect from this moon phase on a personal level.

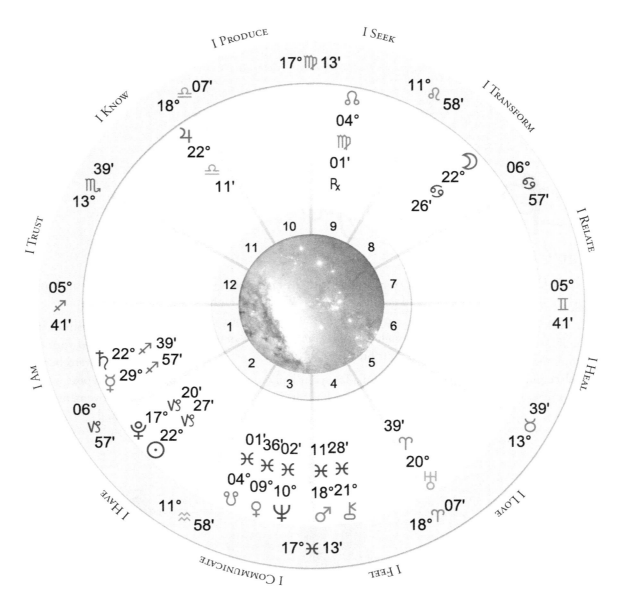

♈	Aries	♋	Cancer	♐	Sagittarius	☽	Moon
♉	Taurus	♌	Leo	♑	Capricorn	☿	Mercury
♊	Gemini	♍	Virgo	♒	Aquarius	♀	Venus
		♎	Libra	♓	Pisces	♂	Mars
		♏	Scorpio	☉	Sun	♃	Jupiter

♄	Saturn	☊	North Node	V/C Void-of-Course
⛢	Uranus	☋	South Node	▲ Super-Sensitivity
♆	Neptune	➡	Enters	▼ Low-Vitality
♇	Pluto	℞	Retrograde	
⚷	Chiron	⚝	Stationary Direct	

Cosmic Check-in

Take a moment to write a brief phrase for each "I" statement. This activates all areas of your life for this creative cycle.

♋ I Feel

♌ I Love

♍ I Heal

♎ I Relate

♏ I Transform

♐ I Seek

♑ I Produce

♒ I Know

♓ I Trust

♈ I Am

♉ I Have

♊ I Communicate

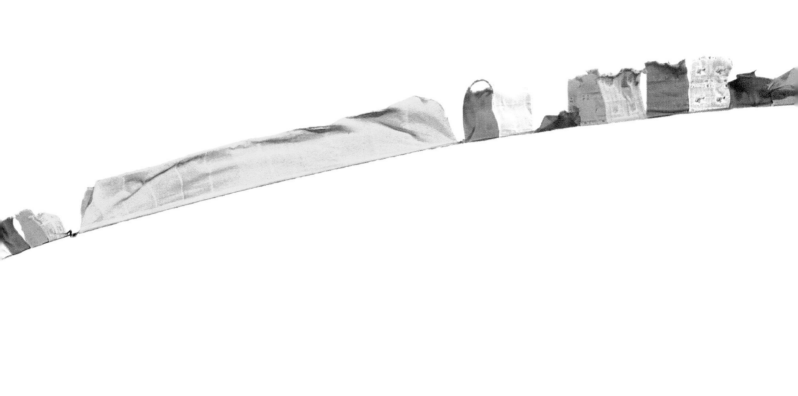

New Moon in Aquarius

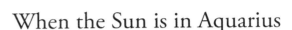

January 27th, 4:07 PM

Statement I Know
Body Ankles
Mind True Genius
Spirit Vision
Element Air – Versatile, expressive, restless, travel-minded, short trips, flirt, gossip, "nose for news," and the messenger.

Degree Choice Points
8° Aquarius 15'
Light Accomplishment
Shadow Pretentiousness
Wisdom Raise the bar for yourself and others.

Seventh House Moon
24° Cancer 34'
Seventh House Umbrella Theme
I Know/I Relate – One-on-one relationships, defines your people attraction force, and how you work in relationships with the people you attract.
Light Credibility
Shadow Deprecation
Wisdom Trust and confidence are restored with new experiences.

Lunar New Year
Beginning at 4:07 PM, the fire rooster brings the dawn of new awakenings, triumph, and success. Success and good fortune are achieved through hard work and taking action towards your goals. The lunar year's yin fire element is magnetic and will increase your inner wisdom, insights, and intuition. Connect with family and friends to enjoy the heart-warming energy of the fire rooster.

When the Sun is in Aquarius

This is a time when the higher octave of the mind comes into play and one is given the power of vision. The Aquarian energies promote knowing by being a wellspring of knowledge. They expand the radius of contact by going beyond the known in areas of communication and cooperation. Now is the time to be initiated into greater awareness to serve the fields of human endeavors. Connect and combine magic with science and become a creative influence. When the sun is in Aquarius we must unify with our team players and collect innovative ideas to advance the world to a better place.

Aquarius Goddess

White Tara steps in to assist you with compassionate acceptance and healing of old, deep wounds that are now illuminated by both the Sun and the Moon. With seven eyes (one on her forehead, one on each hand and each foot), White Tara's ability to see encompasses her ability to feel and connect with others and with the Earth. Her name is derived from the root "tri," which means to cross. She has accepted the task of remaining in feminine form until all beings are enlightened, and is here to help all cross the ocean of existence and suffering.

Call upon White Tara's guidance to navigate towards self-acceptance and self-forgiveness on your path to healing.

Build Your Altar

Colors	Violet, neon, crystalline rainbow tints
Numerology	2 – Make the decision and don't look back
Tarot Card	The Star – Golden opportunities for the future
Gemstones	Aquamarine, blue topaz, peacock pearls
Plant Remedy	Queen of the Night Cactus – Ability to see light in the dark
Fragrance	Myrrh – Healing the nervous system

Aquarius Victories *and* Challenges

Say all of the statements in this section out loud. Then, underline the phrase that means the most to you. Use the phrase as your special affirmation for manifesting throughout this phase of the moon.

Today, I chart my course for my new direction. My future is set on a new, fresh evolutionary course. I am guided by a higher source and trust in that guidance. I know my life has value and I am willing to contribute to the pool of consciousness by experiencing my life and living my life to the fullest view of possibility. Today, I know my possibilities are endless. My Spirit and my Soul are connected to Heaven and to Earth and this knowing brings me to the awareness that I can add to the higher qualities of life because I am connected to the whole. My being is far-reaching and immeasurable. I contribute to existence simply by knowing. All of the guideposts are connected for me today to see my way to a profound new future. My vision is clear and I can clearly set my sights on this new course. Golden opportunities come with this new vision and I trust in my guidance to bring me to this new level of manifesting power. I check in with my inner lights, each day, by meditating and asking for all seven of the energy centers in my body to come into alignment with the outer symbols of guidance. I do this by becoming still and breathing until I feel the stillness. Then, I place my hand on each center in my body, one center at a time, to be activated by light. Next, I ask out loud for each center in my body to let me know what its energetic contribution to the new direction is and how best to use the energy to move forward on my new course of action. I write down each statement and connect each statement to the guiding star in the sky. I am now linked up physically and spiritually and ready to navigate my total self towards my new evolutionary direction.

Aquarius Homework

Aquarians manifest a storehouse of information through innovative telecommunications, technology, social networking and media, and global communication. They are typically found in the fields of psychology, science fiction authoring or film-making, speech writing, and aerospace engineering.

Consider these three Aquarian gifts:

- Opportunity – Become a creative influence
- Enlightenment – When you become aware that you are light
- Brotherhood – Separation doesn't exist anymore

Where do you see these occurring in your life?

Manifesting List

This or something better than this comes to me in an easy and pleasurable way, for the good of all concerned. Thank you, Universe!

Aquarius Manifesting Ideas

Now is the time to focus on manifesting vision, invention, technology, freedom, friends, community, personal genius, higher awareness, teamwork, science, and magic.

Gratitude List

Keep this list active throughout the moon cycle. This will bring you to a level of completion so that a new cycle of opportunity can occur in your life. Be prepared for miracles!

Sky Power Yoga

Elevated Legs

You need two bath towels and one to two pillows for the prop.

Nest two towels together. Fold them lengthwise and roll into a log. Place the towel log on the floor and place your pillow on top for your support prop.

Sit on the floor with your legs straight in front of you and your feet hip-width apart. Place your prop between your feet and then place each foot on the prop.

Sit up straight. Lower yourself onto your elbows and then onto your back. Relax.

Close your eyes. Breathe in and out slowly and deeply several times through your nose with your awareness on your ankles.

Inhale. Say the mantra *I Know* either out loud or in your head.

Exhale softly and slowly. Enjoy breathing with your mantra for a few minutes.

New Moon in Aquarius

How to Use the Moon Book With Your Chart

Fill in the blanks on the Cosmic Check-In page. Then look up the degree of the Moon on the chart below. Take note of the "I" statement on the outside of the wheel where the Moon is located. Now, locate the same degree on your own chart and make a note of the house and corresponding

"I" statement. Go back to the Cosmic Check-In page and circle the two statements from the charts and read what you wrote. This will give you an idea about what to expect from this moon phase on a personal level.

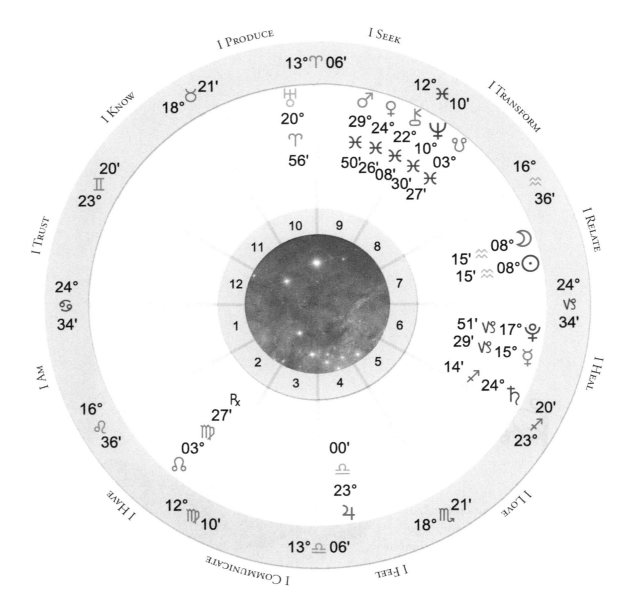

♈	Aries	♋	Cancer	♐	Sagittarius	☽ Moon
♉	Taurus	♌	Leo	♑	Capricorn	☿ Mercury
♊	Gemini	♍	Virgo	♒	Aquarius	♀ Venus
		♎	Libra	♓	Pisces	♂ Mars
		♏	Scorpio	☉	Sun	♃ Jupiter

♄ Saturn	☊ North Node
♅ Uranus	☋ South Node
♆ Neptune	➡ Enters
♇ Pluto	℞ Retrograde
⚷ Chiron	S/D Stationary Direct

V/C Void-of-Course
▲ Super-Sensitivity
▼ Low-Vitality

Cosmic Check-in

Take a moment to write a brief phrase for each "I" statement. This activates all areas of your life for this creative cycle.

♒ I Know

♓ I Trust

♈ I Am

♉ I Have

♊ I Communicate

♋ I Feel

♌ I Love

♍ I Heal

♎ I Relate

♏ I Transform

♐ I Seek

♑ I Produce

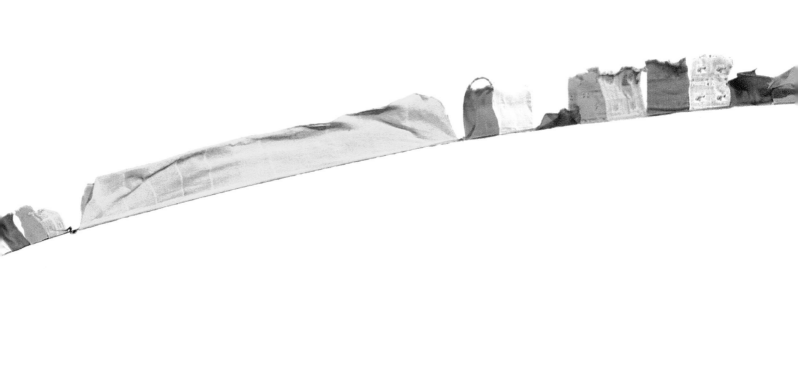

February

Planetary Highlights

Throughout 2017: Jupiter opposite Uranus

Together for the long haul—Jupiter and Uranus influence huge expansion throughout the year. Expand at each end of the opposition by making vastness your friend. Jupiter brings good fortune. Uranus asks for innovative concepts that take us to places where we have not yet ventured. Expand and include so neither separation nor contraction occurs.

February 5-June 9: Jupiter retrograde in Libra

Seek your own truth. Be aware when others invade your space and take you in a different direction.

February 6-7: Low Vitality

Stay centered and balanced as earth changes may stress your life.

February 7: Mercury enters Aquarius

Your genius mind rides on a beam of light. Wake up, surf a new wave, and open your mind to new dimensions to accelerate beyond your wildest dreams.

February 10: Mars conjunct Venus in Aries

Leadership, control, and domination dramas intensify your life. Be patient to avoid brat attacks. If you need immediate gratification, make love not war.

February 13-14: Super Sensitivity

Chaos is in the air. Apply knowledge to tasks that are important and stick to your boundaries. Stay open to receiving rewards as resistance increases problems.

February 18: Sun enters Pisces

Take the high road by following your true spiritual aspirations. Stay in the flow by being aware of your emotions. What is sweet in your life? Concentrate on this sweetness.

February 20-21: Super Sensitivity

Chaos is in the air. Apply knowledge to tasks that are important and stick to your boundaries. Stay open to receiving rewards as resistance increases problems.

February 25: Mercury enters Pisces

Be confident. Speak your truth. Trust your beloveds to accept you as you are.

February 26: Retrograde Jupiter in Libra opposite Uranus and Mars in Aries

The golden opportunity is in letting things be. Know who you are and live your truth despite resistance. The rebel and the warrior may challenge your nobility. Be noble.

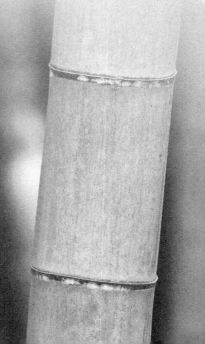

Sunday	Monday	Tuesday	Wednesday	Thursday	Friday	Saturday
			1 7. Don't give your intelligence away.	**2** ☽V/C 8:50AM ☽→♉5:49PM 8. You build on what you trust.	**3** ♀→♈ 7:52AM 9. Caring makes a difference.	**4** ☽V/C 2:41PM ☽→♊ 8:44 PM 10. Don't waste tears on your past.
5 ♃℞ ♃S/D –10:54PM 23° ♎ 08° 2. Stay in balance today.	**6** ♃℞ ▼ ☽V/C 2:53PM ☽→♋ 11:02PM 3. Worry is a misuse of imagination.	**7** ♃℞ ▼ ☿→♒ 2:36AM 4. Build a firm foundation.	**8** ♃℞ ☽V/C 1:59 PM 5. Let the road mark the course of action.	**9** ♃℞ ☽→♌ 1:40 AM 6. Transform truth through expression.	**10** ♃℞ ○22°♌28'4:32PM Lunar Eclipse 4:47PM ☽V/C 9:52PM 7. Sometimes it is best to be silent.	**11** ♃℞ ☽→♍ 5:51 AM 8. Victory requires action.
12 ♃℞ 9. Achievement comes after vision.	**13** ♃℞ ▲ ☽V/C 4:36AM ☽→♎ 12:42PM 10. Release the past and begin anew.	**14** ♃℞ ▲ Valentine's Day 2. Find harmony in partnerships today.	**15** ♃℞ ☽V/C 5:53PM ☽→♏ 10:40 PM 3. Expressing your joy intensifies joy.	**16** ♃℞ 4. Focus creates a proper direction.	**17** ♃℞ ☽V/C 11:37AM 5. Making any change is up to you.	**18** ♃℞ ☽→♐ 10:52 AM ☉→♓ 3:32 AM 6. Love makes your life a safe haven.
19 ♃℞ 7. Be responsible for your mistakes.	**20** ♃℞ ▲ President's Day ☽V/C 3:37PM ☽→♑ 11:07PM 8. Our great wealth is contentment.	**21** ♃℞ ▲ 9. The law of love benefits humanity.	**22** ♃℞ ☽V/C 7:23PM 10. Love can transform foe into friend.	**23** ♃℞ ☽→♒ 9:17AM 2. Take action, complete a decision.	**24** ♃℞ 3. An optimistic view is inspiring.	**25** ♃℞ ☽V/C 10:11AM ☽→♓ 4:24 PM ☿→♓ 3:08 PM 4. To organize will serve you today.
26 ♃℞ ●8°♓12'6:58AM Solar Eclipse 6:56AM 5. Make a difference through action.	**27** ♃℞ ☽V/C 3:07PM ☽→♈ 8:51PM 6. Happiness comes from knowing love.	**28** ♃℞ 7. Be willing to fail so you can achieve.				

♈ Aries	♎ Libra	☉ Sun	♄ Saturn	☊ North Node	▲ Super Sensitivity	6. Love
♉ Taurus	♏ Scorpio	☽ Moon	♅ Uranus	☋ South Node	▼ Low Vitality	7. Learning
♊ Gemini	♐ Sagittarius	☿ Mercury	♆ Neptune	➡ Enters	2. Balance	8. Money
♋ Cancer	♑ Capricorn	♀ Venus	♇ Pluto	℞ Retrograde	3. Fun	9. Spirituality
♌ Leo	♒ Aquarius	♂ Mars	⚷ Chiron	S/D Stationary Direct	4. Structure	10. Visionary
♍ Virgo	♓ Pisces	♃ Jupiter		V/C Void-of-Course	5. Action	11. Completion

Full Moon in Leo

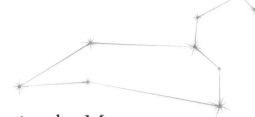

February 10th, 4:32 PM Lunar Eclipse

Statement I Love

Body Heart

Mind Self-confidence

Spirit Generosity

Element Fire – Passionate, enthusiastic, warm, and focused on personal identity.

Degree Choice Points
22° Leo 28'

Light Empowered

Shadow Ill-timed Risk

Wisdom Charge your environment with energy.

First House Moon
11° Leo 16'

First House Umbrella Theme
I Am/I Love – Your outer appearance, the way you present yourself, the way you dress, the way you enter a room, and what you leave behind when you leave the room.

Light Group Relaxation

Shadow Posturing

Wisdom Manifest a goal free of doubt and fear.

The Sun is Opposite the Moon

Full moons are always in opposition to the Sun. This creates a feeling of tension between where you want to shine and how your feelings are flowing on a sensory level about the Sun's directive. The two forces seem like they are working against each other, yet they are on the same team displaying different techniques to obtain the same mission. The Leo/Aquarius polarity creates tension about the need to be adored and the need to be free.

Leo Goddess

The depth of Winter is the dreaming time, when your seed has been planted. The colder temperatures and lack of light naturally draw us inside – within. Rhiannon, the Celtic Goddess, rides her horse through your dreams by night and guides your visions as you stare into the hearth fire. She transverses the liminal space, the doorway between the worlds.

Take a ride with Rhiannon, allowing her to transport you as you do your inner work. Revel in the silence of a quiet night before the fireplace. Find comfort in a hot cup of relaxing herbal tea. Rest and allow yourself a few extra hours of well-deserved sleep!

Build Your Altar

Colors Royal purple, gold, orange

Numerology 7 – Practice silence; the answer is within

Tarot Card Strength – Passion for all of life

Gemstones Amber, emerald, pyrite, citrine, yellow topaz

Plant remedy Sunflower – Standing tall in the center of life

Fragrance Jasmine – Remembering your Soul's original intention

Clearing the Slate

Leo Full Moon – Lunar Eclipse
February 10th
4:32 PM

Sixty hours before the full moon negative traits connected to the astro-sign might become activated to trigger what needs to be released during the full moon phase. You may notice wanting an unusual amount of attention, resistance to authority, or strong impatience that expresses itself as a brat attack. Make a list of the triggers and do Ho'oponopono, a Hawaiian Huna ritual for forgiveness. Look in the mirror, and for each negative trait, tell yourself *I am sorry, I forgive you, thank you for your awareness,* and *I love you.*

Leo Victories and Challenges

Say all of the statements in this section out loud. Then, underline the phrase that means the most to you. Use the phrase as your special affirmation for recalibrating throughout this phase of the moon.

I no longer feel the need to be in control and dominated by my mind telling me that it is appropriate to repress my feelings. I am going to claim my dominion today and feel the power of life running through me. I accept the privilege of being fully human and fully alive. I look to see where I lack courage to connect to what is natural for me. I see where I have been stubborn and turn to face my resistance. I become aware of when my higher self says "Go" and my lower self says "No." I am aware that my lower self (my body) is a creature of habit and will sabotage me with the idea that change takes too much energy. I take responsibility for the part of me that is a creature of habit and talk to my body about coming into alignment with my new intention to become fully passionate and fully alive. I remember today that in order to get the body to move forward with me, I need two-thirds of my cells to align with my request.

First, I become aware of the part of myself that is trying to control all of my outcomes and keep me a slave to those outcomes, rather than trusting in the evolution of nature and the concept of Divine Order. I give up the fight today knowing that this struggle is dissipating all my energy and making me exhausted. In order for my body to respond, I need to awaken my cells through sound and touch. So, today I rub my body and speak out loud by sharing my request for connection, revitalization, rejuvenation, passion, and support. Today, I celebrate the idea that I can connect to my wholeness by activating my cells to support my commitment to my aliveness. I can now stand tall in the center of life and grow in self-confidence.

Leo Homework

Review your memorabilia and see what no longer matches your current love nature, your creative nature, and your loving self. Set your heart free while chanting, "Love is all you need." Become a part of the new consciousness on the Earth that brings a more abundant life when we expand the radius of our love. Live Love Every Day!

Recalibrating List

Say this statement out loud three times before writing your recalibrating list:

I am a free spiritual being and it is my desire to be free to think and to express myself fully.

From this day forward I resolve to be true – first to myself and my highest self, and then to the highest self in me which is the Source of Love That I Am.

Leo Recalibrating Ideas

Now is the time to activate a game change in my life, and give up the need to be the center of attention, obstacles to generosity, false pride, false identity, blocks to confidence or creativity, excuses that keep me from quality time with my children, blocks to knowing that I am loved and lovable, and the idea that everyone needs to be devoted to me in all situations.

Activate Acceleration

By acknowledging what you have recalibrated and overcome, you activate your acceleration. Keep this list active during this moon cycle.

Sky Power Yoga

Reclined Heart Opener

You need two bath towels and one or two pillows for the prop.

Fold the two towels in half lengthwise, roll them into a log, and place them on the floor. Put both pillows on top of the rolled towels to support your back, neck, and head in the pose.

Sit on the floor with the support prop behind you.

Lean back onto your elbows and then lower back onto your support prop. This pose creates a gentle opening

across your chest. If you find your head dangling over the top edge, shift your prop towards your head to support your head and neck fully.

Place your arms out at a 45-degree angle with palms facing upwards at your sides.

Relax. Close your eyes. Breathe in and out slowly and deeply several times

through your nose keeping your awareness on your heart center. Allow your body to soften and relax.

Inhale deeply as you say or think to yourself the mantra *I Love*. Exhale slowly and relax fully into the support prop and the pose. Enjoy breathing with your mantra for a few minutes.

Full Moon in Leo

How to Use the Moon Book With Your Chart

Fill in the blanks on the Cosmic Check-In page. Then look up the degree of the Moon on the chart below. Take note of the "I" statement on the outside of the wheel where the Moon is located. Now, locate the same degree on your own chart and make a note of the house and corresponding

"I" statement. Go back to the Cosmic Check-In page and circle the two statements from the charts and read what you wrote. This will give you an idea about what to expect from this moon phase on a personal level.

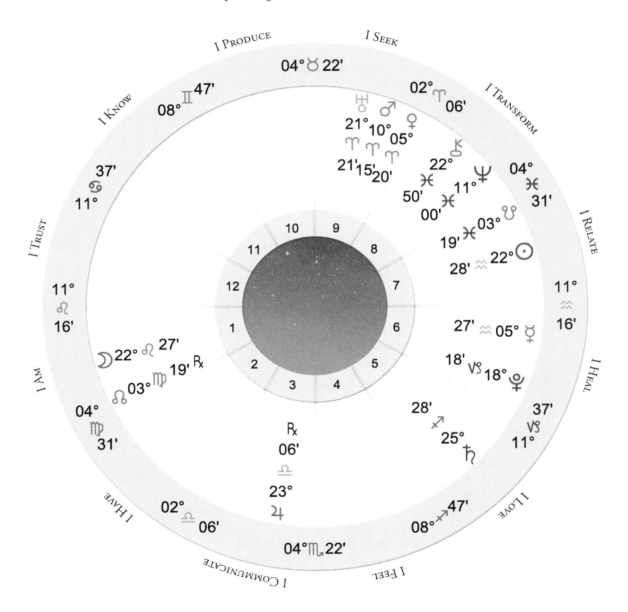

♈	Aries	♋	Cancer	♐	Sagittarius
♉	Taurus	♌	Leo	♑	Capricorn
♊	Gemini	♍	Virgo	♒	Aquarius
		♎	Libra	♓	Pisces
		♏	Scorpio	☉	Sun

☽	Moon	♄	Saturn	☊ North Node
☿	Mercury	♅	Uranus	☋ South Node
♀	Venus	♆	Neptune	➡ Enters
♂	Mars	♇	Pluto	℞ Retrograde
♃	Jupiter	⚷	Chiron	⚡ Stationary Direct

V/C Void-of-Course
▲ Super-Sensitivity
▼ Low-Vitality

Cosmic Check-in

Leo Full Moon – Lunar Eclipse
February 10th
4:32 PM

Take a moment to write a brief phrase for each "I" statement. This activates all areas of your life for this creative cycle.

♌ I Love

♍ I Heal

♎ I Relate

♏ I Transform

♐ I Seek

♑ I Produce

♒ I Know

♓ I Trust

♈ I Am

♉ I Have

♊ I Communicate

♋ I Feel

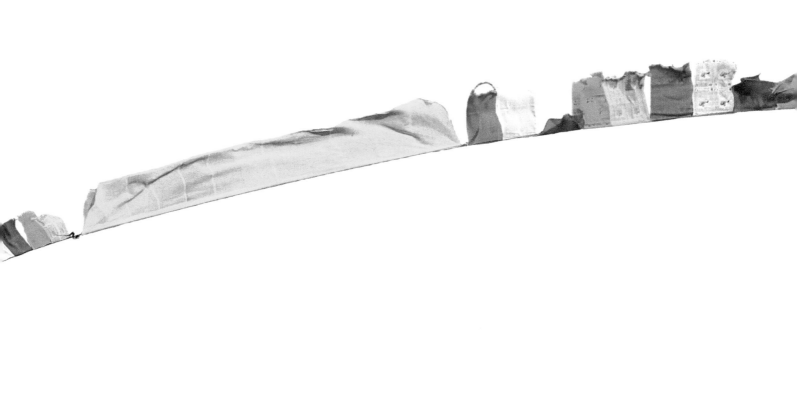

New Moon in Pisces

Statement I Trust

Body Feet

Mind Devotion

Spirit Vastness

Element Water – Sensitive, creative, empathetic, theatrical, glamorous, secretive, divinely guided, the addict, the escape artist, and the healer.

Degree Choice Points

8° Pisces 12'

Light Exhilaration

Shadow Ruthlessness

Wisdom Explore other realms and dimensions.

Twelfth House Moon

14° Aquarius 1'

Twelfth House Umbrella Theme

I Trust/I Know – Determines how you deal with your karma, unconscious software, and what you will experience in order to attain mastery by completing your karma. It is also the way you connect to the Divine.

Light Self-consistency

Shadow Jealousy

Wisdom Reflect the light of wisdom.

Karmic Awakening

Remember the principle of *The I That Is We* in your relationships. Avoid confusion by acknowledging your needs as an individual and the needs of others.

When the Sun is in Pisces

This is a time when you come in contact with your most Divine essence. It is a time to meditate and connect to your higher purpose. Let your intuition guide you to a program of service. Let your Soul take control and connect to a space beyond your ego. In order to do this, you must become free of your habits, hang ups, and fantasies. Compassion frees you from the slavery of self-interest and the lure of your personality's blind urges, emotional traps, and mental crystallizations. When the Soul takes control, you unite your personality with Divine essence and radiate the light needed to find your true pathway.

Pisces Goddess

This new moon, Canola, the Irish mistress of the harp, tugs at your heartstrings. In myth, Canola took a walk after quarrelling with her lover one night, and fell asleep outdoors to hypnotic music. The next morning she awoke to find that it was the sound of the wind passing through the sinews of a whale carcass; from this she invented the harp.

Trust the messages that come to you through song. Take a break to breathe, chant, and sing to your heart's content, knowing that the sound will carry your will and intention, with beauty, harmony, and balance, into the world, healing yourself and others. Bring the spring plants to life with your voice!

Build Your Altar

Colors Turquoise, blue, green, aqua

Numerology 5 – Make a difference through your actions

Tarot Card The Moon – The inner journey, reflection, illumination

Gemstones Amethyst, opal, jade, turquoise

Plant Remedy Passion flower – The ability to live in the here and now

Fragrance Lotus – Connecting to the Divine without arrogance

Pisces Victories and Challenges

Say all of the statements in this section out loud. Then, underline the phrase that means the most to you. Use the phrase as your special affirmation for manifesting throughout this phase of the moon.

I see my path clearly now. I know I must walk by myself on this journey into the deepest part of my Soul. It is time to clear the way and look beneath the surface to discover the parts of myself that I have placed in the unconscious world to be worked on at a later date. That later date is now. I am aware that the postponement of my inner reality can no longer be delayed.

Evolution is pulling me and it has become greater than my distractions, my fear, my denial, and my refusal to face what I have hidden from myself and others. I am aware of outside influences that pull me away from facing my inner realms. I know, without a doubt, that I am only as sick as the secrets I keep from myself and others. I see clearly how these distractions, illusions, and secrets need to be recognized so I can find the separated parts of myself that have been left in the dark, obscured from the light. I know that it is time to bring myself into wholeness and bring my shadow side to the light of my awareness.

I begin by closing my eyes and experiencing darkness. I imagine walking on a lonely road, in the dark, by myself. I pay particular attention to the sensations in my body and allow for the body to guide me to the places of dullness, numbness, fear, and anxiety. I simply allow for the intelligence of the body to coordinate the feeling with an image, person, or an event. I stay still and know, from the depth of my being, that recognition is all that is required of me right now. When recognition occurs, the light of awareness is ignited and the conscious world will take care of the rest. I know that the road to enlightenment requires me to first take the road into the dark side of my Soul.

Pisces Homework

Pisces manifest by using their psychic powers for counseling, therapy, hypnosis, the ministry, and creating spiritual schools or healing centers. They are also successful in visionary arts, acting, music, medical and pharmaceutical fields, and oceanography.

Take time to go within to discover where new pathways are open for advancement. Blessings pour forth to those who move toward these pathways in the spirit of service. Be open to these pathways and consider the ones that benefit our planet with new ideas, creative expression, and expanded views that lead people to higher levels of service.

Manifesting List

This or something better than this comes to me in an easy and pleasurable way, for the good of all concerned. Thank you, Universe!

Pisces Manifesting Ideas

Now is the time to focus on manifesting connection with the Divine, creativity, healing powers, psychic abilities, sensitivity, compassion, and service.

Gratitude List

Keep this list active throughout the moon cycle. This will bring you to a level of completion so that a new cycle of opportunity can occur in your life. Be prepared for miracles!

Sky Power Yoga

Seated Foot Flex

You need one chair for the prop.

With a straight back sit in a chair with your feet on the floor hip-width apart. Feet should have solid contact with the floor. Use pillows or folded towels to support your feet, if necessary.

Bring your right foot forward.

Relax. Close your eyes. Breathe in and out slowly and deeply several times through your nose with your awareness on your feet.

Point your right toe. Inhale deeply.

Say the mantra *I Trust* either out loud or in your head. Then pause and lift only your toes.

Exhale and flex your whole foot.

Relax and breathe. Repeat three times and change legs.

45

New Moon in Pisces

How to Use the Moon Book With Your Chart

Fill in the blanks on the Cosmic Check-In page. Then look up the degree of the Moon on the chart below. Take note of the "I" statement on the outside of the wheel where the Moon is located. Now, locate the same degree on your own chart and make a note of the house and corresponding

"I" statement. Go back to the Cosmic Check-In page and circle the two statements from the charts and read what you wrote. This will give you an idea about what to expect from this moon phase on a personal level.

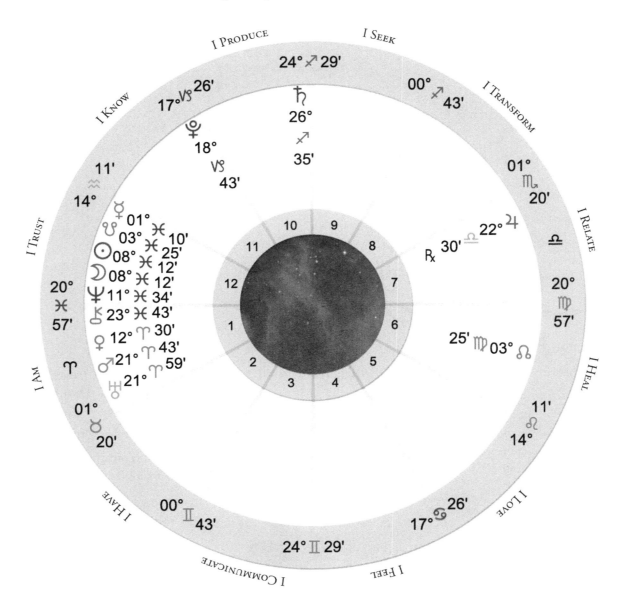

♈	Aries	♋	Cancer	♐	Sagittarius	☽ Moon
♉	Taurus	♌	Leo	♑	Capricorn	☿ Mercury
♊	Gemini	♍	Virgo	♒	Aquarius	♀ Venus
		♎	Libra	♓	Pisces	♂ Mars
		♏	Scorpio	☉	Sun	♃ Jupiter

♄	Saturn	☊ North Node	V/C Void-of-Course
♅	Uranus	☋ South Node	▲ Super-Sensitivity
♆	Neptune	➡ Enters	▼ Low-Vitality
♇	Pluto	℞ Retrograde	
⚷	Chiron	S/D Stationary Direct	

Cosmic Check-in

Take a moment to write a brief phrase for each "I" statement. This activates all areas of your life for this creative cycle.

♓ I Trust

♈ I Am

♉ I Have

♊ I Communicate

♋ I Feel

♌ I Love

♍ I Heal

♎ I Relate

♏ I Transform

♐ I Seek

♑ I Produce

♒ I Know

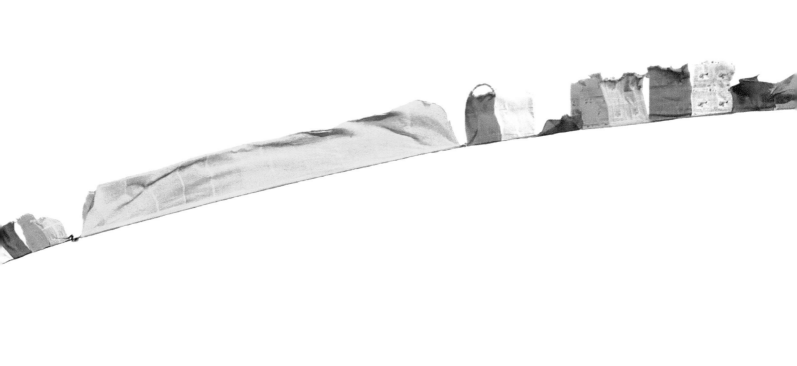

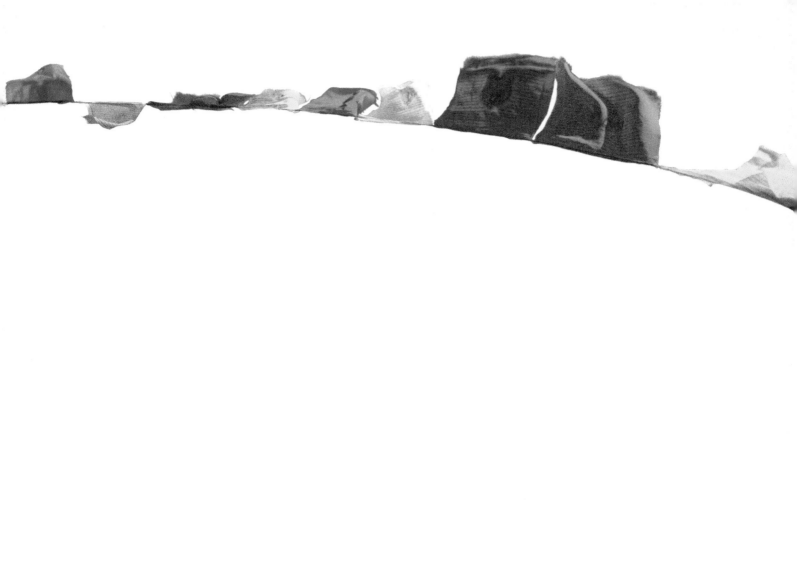

March

Planetary Highlights

Until June 9: Jupiter retrograde in Libra

Review the year 2005, by asking yourself: With whom was I in relationship? Where did I give my power away? How would I do it differently now?

March 4-April 15: Venus retrograde in Aries

Desire, its impulses, and the need for immediate gratification increase in an uncontrollable manner. Brat attacks could get out of control.

March 6-7: Low Vitality

Earth changes are possible as energy is not available. Let be and get rest as forcing anything could deplete you.

March 9: Mars enters Taurus

Slow down and smell the roses. Take time for luxury as rushing ruins everything.

March 13: Mercury enters Aries

Acceleration is happening in your thought world. Write down your ideas to take advantage of innovations that will get you everywhere. Put your thoughts into action.

March 20: Spring Equinox—Sun enters Aries

Celebrate astrology's new year! Every blade of grass has been awakened from winter's sleep and dream time is over. Let inspiration guide you to your new assignment.

March 31: Mercury enters Taurus

Manifest your thoughts into reality by adding your light into physical forms.

March 12: Sun, Chiron, and Mercury tripled in Pisces

New directions and pathways lead to innovative ideas and methodologies especially in healing and spiritual practices.

March 17: Retrograde Jupiter in Libra opposite Uranus in Aries

Recalibrate rebellious relationships to express the truth. Use freedom rather than rebellion to relate peacefully.

March 20-22: Super Sensitivity

All will be well if you leave chaotic and disruptive energy alone and stay away from what doesn't belong to you.

March 25: Mercury and Uranus coupled in Aries

Pay attention as your mind could bring in a new approach for the future.

March 27: Moon, Sun, and Venus tripled in Aries

Express your self-esteem from a place of inner awareness. If you look for direction from outside, it could backfire.

March 27: Retrograde Jupiter in Libra conjunct the Ascendant

Expect a major acceleration from a true point of power. Let that power take you for a ride.

March 27: South Node conjunct Pisces

Say good-bye to old belief systems. Lighten your load by letting go of hidden emotions that have outlived their usefulness.

Sunday	Monday	Tuesday	Wednesday	Thursday	Friday	Saturday
			1 ♃℞ ☽V/C 6:18 PM ☽→♉ 11:42 PM 8. Joyfully share what you have.	2 ♃℞ 9. Know that you are divinely blessed.	3 ♃℞ ☽V/C 7:20 AM 10. Use acceleration for change.	4 ♀♃℞ ☽→♊ 2:05 AM ♀SR—1:10AM 13°♈08' 2. Be steady and stay in balance.
5 ♀♃℞ 3. Your experiences bring in joy today.	6 ♀♃℞ ▼ ☽V/C 12:21AM ☽→♋ 4:54 AM 4. Be practical in thought and action.	7 ♀♃℞ ▼ 5. Take a risk and be adventurous.	8 ♀♃℞ ☽V/C 6:59 AM ☽→♌ 8:45 AM 6. Just for fun, send someone a card.	9 ♀♃℞ ♂→♉4:35PM 7. Take a class in something new.	10 ♀♃℞ ☽V/C 9:05AM ☽→♍ 2:07 PM 8. Being rich isn't just about money.	11 ♀♃℞ 9. Donate to your favorite charity.
12 ♀♃℞ PDT Begins ○ 22°♍13' 7:53AM ☽V/C 7:36PM ☽→♎ 10:28 PM 10. Plan a long awaited trip.	13 ♀♃℞ ☿→♈2:08PM 2. Look at both sides of an issue.	14 ♀♃℞ 3. Use your ability to make it fun.	15 ♀♃℞ ☽V/C 3:05AM ☽→♏ 8:10 AM 5. Change is good for the spirit.	16 ♀♃℞ 6. Plan and create a dinner party.	17 ♀♃℞ St. Patrick's Day ☽V/C 2:56 PM ☽→♐ 7:59 PM 7. You always know the answer within.	18 ♀♃℞ 8. Feel successful and strong today.
19 ♀♃ 9. Where love is - miracles happen.	20 ♀♃ ▲ ☽V/C 3:37AM ☽→♑ 8:30 AM Spring Equinox ☉→♈3:30AM 10. Live fully in the now.	21 ♀♃ ▲ 2. A sense of wellbeing creates balance.	22 ♀♃ ☽V/C 6:19AM ☽→♒ 7:28 PM 3. Call your friends and have a party.	23 ♀♃ 4. An organized approach is best.	24 ♀♃ ☽V/C 10:55 PM 5. Everything you do affects the world.	25 ♀♃ ☽→♓ 3:06 AM 6. Trust love and all will be well.
26 ♀♃℞ 7. Look at the big picture.	27 ♀♃℞ ● 7°♈37' 7:57PM ☽V/C 3:19 AM ☽→♈ 7:10 AM 8. Generosity requires boundaries.	28 ♀♃℞ 9. Pray for happiness and all will be well.	29 ♀♃℞ ☽V/C 5:06 AM ☽→♉ 8:47 AM 10. When it's over, let it be.	30 ♀♃℞ ☽V/C 4:12PM 2. Back decisions with action.	31 ♀♃℞ ☽→♊ 9:40 AM ☿→♉10:32 AM 3. Creativity creates your joy.	

♈ Aries	♎ Libra	☉ Sun	♄ Saturn	☊ North Node	▲ Super Sensitivity	6. Love
♉ Taurus	♏ Scorpio	☽ Moon	♅ Uranus	☋ South Node	▼ Low Vitality	7. Learning
♊ Gemini	♐ Sagittarius	☿ Mercury	♆ Neptune	➡ Enters	2. Balance	8. Money
♋ Cancer	♑ Capricorn	♀ Venus	♇ Pluto	℞ Retrograde	3. Fun	9. Spirituality
♌ Leo	♒ Aquarius	♂ Mars	⚷ Chiron	S/D Stationary Direct	4. Structure	10. Visionary
♍ Virgo	♓ Pisces	♃ Jupiter		V/C Void-of-Course	5. Action	11. Completion

Full Moon in Virgo

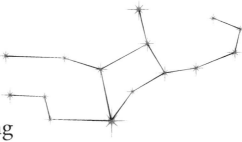

March 12th, 7:53 AM

Statement I Heal

Body Intestines

Mind Critical

Spirit Divinity in the Details

Element Earth – The way you manage your body and appearance. Family lineage and DNA healing, knowing abundance, healing power from the plant kingdom and nutrition, body awareness, and connection to small animals.

Degree Choice Points
22° Virgo 12'

Light Professionalism

Shadow Indispensability

Wisdom Variety is important to your progress.

First House Moon
29° Leo 19'

First House Umbrella Theme
I Heal /I Love – The way you manage your body and appearance.

Light Leadership

Shadow Indiscretion

Wisdom Passion motivates you to take action.

Karmic Awakening

Over-analyzing which healing protocol to adopt may lead to confusion. Simply trust that you will know which option is best. Open your inner wisdom and encourage the healing to begin.

The Sun is Opposite the Moon

Full moons are always in opposition to the Sun. This creates a feeling of tension between where you want to shine and how your feelings are flowing on a sensory level about the Sun's directive. The two forces seem like they are working against each other, yet they are on the same team displaying different techniques to obtain the same mission. The Virgo/Pisces polarity creates tension between doing your work and finding your path.

Virgo Goddess

Astraea is the virgin Goddess of Purity, who fled the Earth upon seeing weaponry, warfare, and the rise of patriarchy that destroyed the earth goddess culture during the Iron Age. She ascended to the heavens to become the constellation Virgo, to watch over the Earth until she will one day return issuing in a new Utopian age. Often depicted as a star maiden, she has wings and a shining halo or crown of stars, and carries a flaming torch or thunderbolt.

Ask Astraea to help you as you sort through the details to bring love and light into a fresh new perspective, free from the restrictions of the past. "Because it's always been done that way," is no longer a viable excuse. Sharing what you love, with the intention for the highest and best for all, enlists Astraea's blessings.

Build Your Altar

Colors Green, blue, earth tones

Numerology 10 – Plan a long-awaited trip

Tarot Card The Hermit – Knowing your purpose and sharing it with the world

Gemstones Emerald, sapphire

Plant remedy Sage – The ability to hold and store light

Fragrance Lavender – Management and storage of energy

Clearing the Slate

Sixty hours before the full moon negative traits connected to the astro-sign might become activated to trigger what needs to be released during the full moon phase. You may notice an extreme sense of judgement, an obsession for detail, or letting perfectionism stop your action. Make a list of the triggers and do Ho'oponopono, a Hawaiian Huna ritual for forgiveness. Look in the mirror, and for each negative trait, tell yourself *I am sorry, I forgive you, thank you for your awareness,* and *I love you.*

Virgo Victories and Challenges

Say all of the statements in this section out loud. Then, underline the phrase that means the most to you. Use the phrase as your special affirmation for recalibrating throughout this phase of the moon.

Today I take time to go within to be silent. I imagine myself on a country road moving towards a beautiful mountain. I bask in the glory of the power of the mountain and know that it is calling me to the top. I find a pathway to the top and begin to climb. As I climb I become aware of a presence guiding me and empowering me to keep going, creating a sense of peacefulness within me.

I become aware of my own power in this silent journey to the top and revel in the serenity that nature and silence bring me. At last I am about to reach the summit and, just before I do, I feel the power drawing me to go within on a deeper level. I stop for a moment and look back at the path I have just climbed and know that my life's path is a remarkable gift. I connect to the center of the Earth and feel an inner glow.

The top of the mountain calls to me and, as I reach the top, a voice says to me, "Take in the view and look in all directions." As I turn 360-degrees, I sense a light igniting me in every direction. Then the voice says, "Look up!" Now, my awareness shifts and I see that I have become an illuminating light glowing in all six directions. Next I hear, "Sit in your silence and take in the vastness of who you are. Who you are is immeasurable." I sit, feeling the glow of light within me, and become aware of a greater plan for my life. I allow myself to receive this plan. I accept this assignment and slowly walk down the mountain, knowing that I can be a shining light for myself and others. I know I must take my light out to the world and share what I know to be my truth. Today, I become a messenger for the light.

Virgo Homework

Become integrated so that the light of your personality becomes soul-infused. When you are soul-infused and are in service to your Higher Self, you radiate love and light through the power of the inner self through all activities, thoughts, and emotions and become more magnificent. Learn the art of detachment and let your Soul take control.

Recalibrating List

Say this statement out loud three times before writing your recalibrating list:

I am a free spiritual being and it is my desire to be free to think and to express myself fully.

I hereby fully and completely free my mind from all adhesions to outdated philosophies, habits, relationships, groups of people, man-made laws, moral codes, all rules, set ideas and set ways of thinking, traditions, organizations, duty-motivated activities, guilt, judgment, and being misunderstood!

Virgo Recalibrating Ideas

Now is the time to activate a game change in my life, and give up finding fault with myself, my addiction to perfection, my addiction to detail, over-indulging in image management, pain-producing thinking patterns, judgment of others, resistance to being healthy, and destructive behaviors.

Activate Acceleration

By acknowledging what you have recalibrated and overcome, you activate your acceleration. Keep this list active during this moon cycle.

Sky Power Yoga

Prone Spinal Twist

You need two bath towels and one pillow for the prop.

Nest the two towels, fold in half lengthwise, and roll them into a log. Place the towel log on the floor with the pillow on top for your support prop.

Sit on your side with your right hip on the floor. Place your support prop at a 90-degree angle to your thigh.

Inhale anchoring your sitting bones to the floor and lengthening your spine.

Exhale and gently lower your upper torso down onto the prop. Your gaze is the same direction as your knees. This creates a subtle restorative twist. Walk your hands forward in order to release your shoulders.

Relax. Close your eyes. Breathe in and out slowly and deeply several times through your nose with your awareness on your intestines.

Inhale deeply as you say or think to yourself the mantra *I Heal*.

Exhale slowly and relax more deeply into the pose.

Breathe with your mantra for a few minutes before repeating on the opposite side.

Full Moon in Virgo

How to Use the Moon Book With Your Chart

Fill in the blanks on the Cosmic Check-In page. Then look up the degree of the Moon on the chart below. Take note of the "I" statement on the outside of the wheel where the Moon is located. Now, locate the same degree on your own chart and make a note of the house and corresponding

"I" statement. Go back to the Cosmic Check-In page and circle the two statements from the charts and read what you wrote. This will give you an idea about what to expect from this moon phase on a personal level.

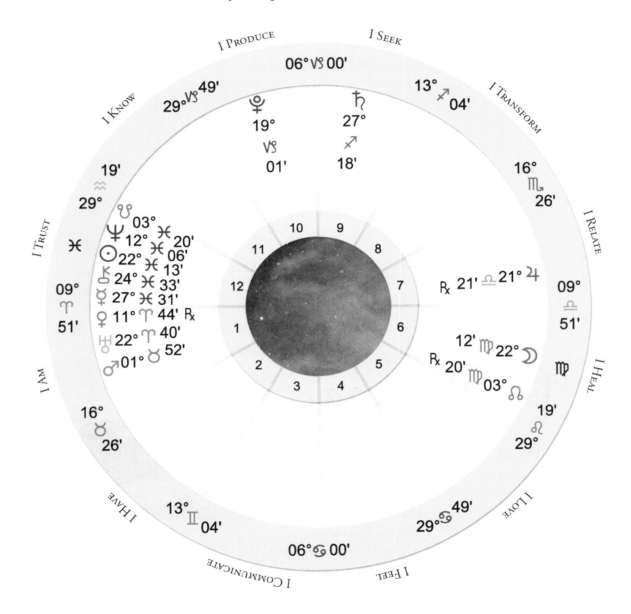

♈	Aries	♋	Cancer	✗
♉	Taurus	♌	Leo	♑
♊	Gemini	♍	Virgo	♒

✗	Sagittarius	☽	Moon
♑	Capricorn	☿	Mercury
♒	Aquarius	♀	Venus
♓	Pisces	♂	Mars
☉	Sun	♃	Jupiter

♄	Saturn	☊	North Node
♅	Uranus	☋	South Node
♆	Neptune	➡	Enters
♇	Pluto	℞	Retrograde
⚷	Chiron	S/D	Stationary Direct

V/C	Void-of-Course
▲	Super-Sensitivity
▼	Low-Vitality

56

Cosmic Check-in

Take a moment to write a brief phrase for each "I" statement. This activates all areas of your life for this creative cycle.

♍ I Heal

♎ I Relate

♏ I Transform

♐ I Seek

♑ I Produce

♒ I Know

♓ I Trust

♈ I Am

♉ I Have

♊ I Communicate

♋ I Feel

♌ I Love

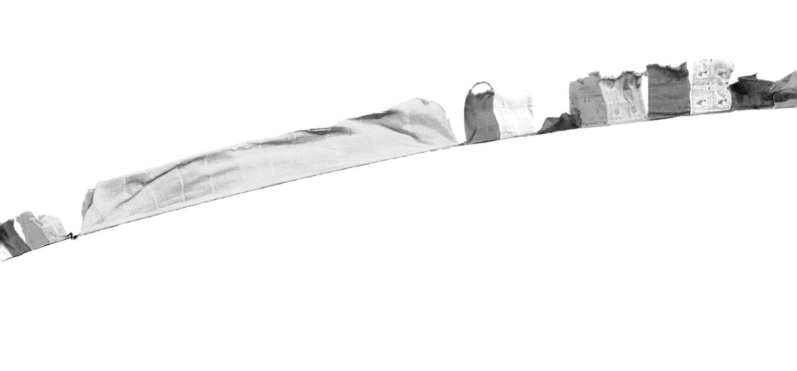

New Moon in Aries

March 27th, 7:57 PM

Statement I Am
Body Head
Mind Impulsive
Spirit Initiation
Element Fire – Ego, identity, championship, leadership, action-oriented, self-first, the warrior, the divine masculine.

Degree Choice Points
7° Aries 36'
Light Guided by Spirit
Shadow Posing
Wisdom Everything is experience—there is no positive or negative.

Sixth House Moon
23° Pisces 24'
Sixth House Umbrella Theme
I Heal /I Am – The way you manage your body and appearance.
Light Revelation
Shadow Pollution
Wisdom Completing a blueprint requirement feels like a mini-death.

When the Sun is in Aries

Aries awakens the dreamer from Winter sleep and represents the raw energy of Spring, when the new shoots of life burst forth. Aries is the fundamental, straightforward approach to life. There is no challenge that is too great, no obstacle too daunting, and no rival too powerful for the Aries. Aries symbolizes initiation, leadership, strength, and potency. Competition and achievement are very important to Aries. Now is the time to be a pioneer and break all barriers to become the winner you are.

Aries Goddess

Pandora was created by Zeus, who was angry about Prometheus stealing the secret of fire. She was the first human woman, whose name means "the all-giving." The gods all conspired to each invest her with seductive gifts. Hesiod's story tells us that Pandora's curiosity led her to open a jar (not a box) that unleashed evils upon humanity. However, Pandora, also known as Anesidora, "she who sends up gifts" from the Earth, could instead be interpreted as opening the pithos (the vessel), an ancient symbol of the Divine Feminine, and generously gifting the world with fertility and creativity.

As you reinterpret your identity this moon, ask Pandora to help you get curious and creative about the "I" you present to the world and how that contributes to the "We."

Build Your Altar

Colors Red, black, white
Numerology 8 – Generosity keeps prosperity alive
Tarot Card Emperor – Success on all levels
Gemstones Diamond, red jasper, coral, obsidian
Plant Remedy Pomegranates, oak – Planting new life and rooting new life
Fragrance Ginger – The ability to ingest and digest life

Aries Victories and Challenges

Say all of the statements in this section out loud. Then, underline the phrase that means the most to you. Use the phrase as your special affirmation for manifesting throughout this phase of the moon.

I am the author of my life. I accept that I am a winner and, in so doing, all doors are open to me. I hold the world in the palm of my hand and I know that there is not a mountain that I cannot climb. My ability to respond to life is in operation today and I direct my intention to bring me to the next level of self-determined achievement. The world and its systems are available for me to use as tools for my success and I use them with true excellence. I am organized and all systems are in place for me to make my mark on the world. I accept that my structured ground state and my dynamic energy are ready to make headway using pure determination, action, planning, and power. I will manage this plan and know that the sequence of events provided support me to make a breakthrough today.

I am willing to make my plan and take action on it. I gather my support team together today to focus on the appropriate action and encourage each person in their area of excellence and production. I am a great leader and my dynamic power is a good resource for others to determine their own success formula. I am aware that all parts of my team are important and place value on all areas of performance required to manifest in the world. I know how to place people in their best areas of expertise, so they can experience their own unique talent manifesting. Today, I honor my father for what he taught me by what he did, or didn't do, to encourage my ability to perform. I am the producer. I am the protector. I am the provider. I am the promoter. I am power. I am the author of my life.

Aries Homework

Aries manifest best through sales and promotions, and as a professional athlete, personal trainer or coach, martial arts expert, military professional, demolition expert, fireworks manufacturer, or wardrobe consultant.

Merge your light and dark forces so balance can occur. Then, give shape to your feelings through creative forms and learn to live in the duality of your Soul and watch your spirit soar! The embodiment of this duality connects you to the Unity, a requirement for these times.

Manifesting List

This or something better than this comes to me in an easy and pleasurable way, for the good of all concerned. Thank you, Universe!

Aries Manifesting Ideas

Now is the time to focus on manifesting personality power, leadership, strength, self-acceptance, winning, courage, personal appearance, and advancing to new frontiers.

Gratitude List

Keep this list active throughout the moon cycle. This will bring you to a level of completion so that a new cycle of opportunity can occur in your life. Be prepared for miracles!

Sky Power Yoga

Mountain Pose

No props are needed.

Stand with your feet hip-width apart. Lift your toes, spread them wide, and place them back on the floor.

To massage the bottoms of your feet, rock back and forth and side to side for 30 seconds. Gradually make your movements more subtle until you find the sweet spot where your weight is balanced evenly across your feet.

Squeeze your thighs to lift your kneecaps. Slightly tuck your tailbone down and feel your hips align over your ankles.

Inhale, lengthening your spine. Exhale, rolling your shoulders back and down, reaching your fingertips towards the floor. Gently lift your chest from the sternum and turn your palms out slightly. Imagine a strong line of vertical energy running from the bottom of your feet to the top of your head.

Relax into the pose. Close your eyes. Breathe in and out slowly and deeply several times through your nose with your awareness on your head.

Inhale deeply. Envision the energy of your breath coming up from the earth into your feet, up your legs, up your spine, and out the top of your head.

Say or think to yourself the mantra *I Am*. Exhale slowly. Envision the breath returning back into your head, down your spine, down your legs, out your feet and back into the earth. Repeat as desired.

New Moon in Aries

How to Use the Moon Book With Your Chart

Fill in the blanks on the Cosmic Check-In page. Then look up the degree of the Moon on the chart below. Take note of the "I" statement on the outside of the wheel where the Moon is located. Now, locate the same degree on your own chart and make a note of the house and corresponding

"I" statement. Go back to the Cosmic Check-In page and circle the two statements from the charts and read what you wrote. This will give you an idea about what to expect from this moon phase on a personal level.

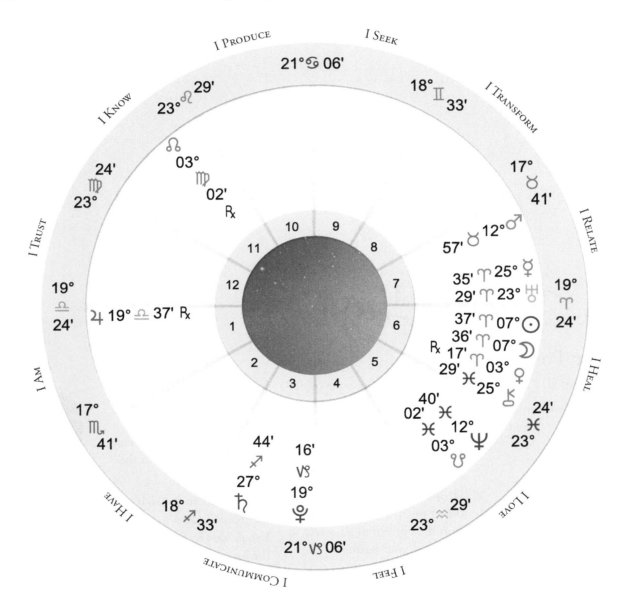

♈	Aries	♋	Cancer	♐	Sagittarius	☽	Moon	♄	Saturn	☊	North Node	V/C Void-of-Course
♉	Taurus	♌	Leo	♑	Capricorn	☿	Mercury	♅	Uranus	☋	South Node	▲ Super-Sensitivity
♊	Gemini	♍	Virgo	♒	Aquarius	♀	Venus	♆	Neptune	➡	Enters	▼ Low-Vitality
		♎	Libra	♓	Pisces	♂	Mars	♇	Pluto	℞	Retrograde	
		♏	Scorpio	☉	Sun	♃	Jupiter	⚷	Chiron	S/D	Stationary Direct	

Cosmic Check-in

Take a moment to write a brief phrase for each "I" statement. This activates all areas of your life for this creative cycle.

♈ I Am

♉ I Have

♊ I Communicate

♋ I Feel

♌ I Love

♍ I Heal

♎ I Relate

♏ I Transform

♐ I Seek

♑ I Produce

♒ I Know

♓ I Trust

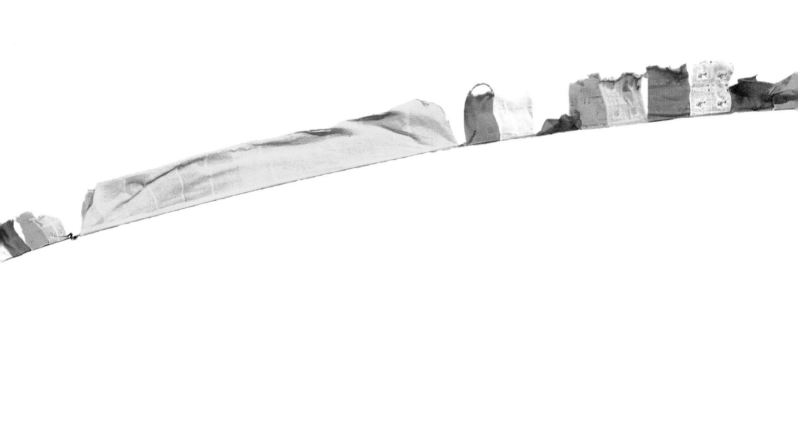

April

Planetary Highlights

Until June 9: Jupiter retrograde in Libra

Add beauty into your space to un-stress your life. Upgrades, such as flowers, new fabrics, and anything fun, make recalibration easier.

Until April 15: Venus retrograde in Pisces

Move beyond rose-colored glasses to see what romance actually provides rather than living in a fantasy world.

April 2: Venus enters Pisces

Get juicy! Romance is in the air.

April 2-3: Low Vitality

Get rest, stay close to home, and remember if an energy field is ending, let it end.

April 5-August 25: Saturn retrograde in Sagittarius

Face the downside of Sagittarius's tendency towards excessiveness and exaggeration. Recalibrate and rebalance with the help of Saturn.

April 9-May 3: Mercury retrograde in Taurus

If you shop, you may return everything the next day! Clean your closets and your yard instead.

April 10: Moon and Jupiter dance

Open to the dance and accelerate your abundance!

April 10: Retrograde Venus in Chiron

The feminine receives a major healing from the collective energy.

April 10: Sun and Uranus conjunct in Aries

Accelerate your ability to connect consciously with what's next for you. Get out your journal, write down your goals, and take action on your future now.

April 16-17: Super Sensitivity

To avoid making choices that you might regret later, avoid chaos as it could play havoc with your nerves.

April 19: Sun enters Taurus

Hit the ground, get your feet moving, and dance your life! If the lap of luxury offers you a seat, take it.

April 20: Mercury retrograde enters Aries

If you back up your thoughts with action, manifestation will happen.

April 20-September 28: Pluto retrograde in Capricorn

Get down to the bones of your issues related to money and security. Make choices beyond survival to bring abundance into your life.

April 21: Mars enters Gemini

Expect speed. The acceleration is zero to ninety in seconds!

April 26: Mercury and Uranus coupled in Aries

Honor new directions in your life by speaking up and sharing your ideas and goals.

April 28: Venus enters Aries

Immediate gratification or brat attacks—the choice is yours.

April 29-30: Low Vitality

Get rest, stay close to home, and remember if an energy field is ending, let it end.

Sunday	Monday	Tuesday	Wednesday	Thursday	Friday	Saturday
						1 ☿♃℞ 4. Be a grounded & positive influence.
2 ☿♃℞▼ ☽V/C 7:42AM ☽→♋11:26AM ♀→♓5:26PM 5. Live a life full of variety.	**3** ☿♃℞▼ 6. Planting kindness gathers love.	**4** ☿♃℞ ☽V/C1:45PM ☽→♌ 3:13PM 7. Asking why solves problems.	**5** ☿♃♄℞ ♄℞27°♐47′10:07PM 8. Gratitude creates abundance.	**6** ☿♃♄℞ ☽V/C 5:16 PM ☽→♍ 9:19 PM 9. Prayers center your purpose.	**7** ☿♃♄℞ 10. Choice with intent transforms.	**8** ☿♃♄℞ 2. Respect all opinions.
9 ☿☿♃♄℞ ☽V/C 1:21AM ☽→♎ 5:34AM ☿℞– 4:15 PM 4°♉50′ 3. Individual freedom is for all.	**10** ☿☿♃♄℞ Passover ○21°♎33′11:08PM 4. You are loyal and down-to-earth.	**11** ☿☿♃♄℞ ☽V/C 11:18AM ☽→♏ 3:41PM 5. Make smart changes.	**12** ☿☿♃♄℞ 6. Base relationships on love, not need.	**13** ☿☿♃♄℞ ☽V/C 9:17PM 7. Education is a gift to benefit all.	**14** ☿☿♃♄℞ ☽→♐3:26AM 8. Self-reliance is the new authority.	**15** ☿♃♄℞ ☿℞—3:19AM 26°♓54′ 9. Be generous with your time.
16 ☿♃♄℞▲ Easter ☽V/C 11:26 AM ☽→♑ 4:04 PM 10. Support the rise of high aspirations.	**17** ☿♃♄℞▲ 2. See where you can agree.	**18** ☿♃♄℞ 3. Turn on the music and dance.	**19** ☿♃♄℞ ☽V/C 2:56 AM ☽→♒ 3:51 AM ☉→♉ 2:28 PM 4. Organize a cluttered space.	**20** ☿♃♄♇℞ ♇℞—5:46AM 19°♑23′ ☿→♈10:38AM 5. What can you do differently?	**21** ☿♃♄♇℞ ☽V/C 11:22 AM ☽→♓ 12:42 PM ♂→♊ 3:33 AM 6. Plant some flowers today.	**22** ☿♃♄♇℞ 7. Be surprised by your deep thought.
23 ☿♃♄♇℞ ☽V/C 2:34 PM ☽→♈ 5:32 PM 8. Have the courage to act on ambition.	**24** ☿♃♄♇℞ 9. Doing your best is enough.	**25** ☿♃♄♇℞ ☽V/C 2:53 PM ☽→♉ 6:56 PM 10. Allow for enlightenment.	**26** ☿♃♄♇℞ ●6°♉27′5:16AM 2. Balance occurs with loving service.	**27** ☿♃♄♇℞ ☽V/C 6:18 PM ☽→♊ 6:38 PM 3. Being creative has many facets.	**28** ☿♃♄♇℞ ♀→♈ 6:14 AM 4. Stability is in the common ground.	**29** ☿♃♄♇℞▼ ☽V/C 2:28 PM ☽→♋ 6:47 PM 5. Be willing to change as needed.
30 ☿♃♄♇℞▼ 6. Relationships are love in present time.						

♈ Aries	♎ Libra	☉ Sun	♄ Saturn	☊ North Node	▲ Super Sensitivity	6. Love
♉ Taurus	♏ Scorpio	☽ Moon	♅ Uranus	☋ South Node	▼ Low Vitality	7. Learning
♊ Gemini	♐ Sagittarius	☿ Mercury	♆ Neptune	➡ Enters	2. Balance	8. Money
♋ Cancer	♑ Capricorn	♀ Venus	♇ Pluto	℞ Retrograde	3. Fun	9. Spirituality
♌ Leo	♒ Aquarius	♂ Mars	⚷ Chiron	S/D Stationary Direct	4. Structure	10. Visionary
♍ Virgo	♓ Pisces	♃ Jupiter		V/C Void-of-Course	5. Action	11. Completion

Full Moon in Libra

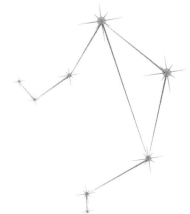

April 10th, 11:08 PM

Statement I Relate
Body Kidneys
Mind Social
Spirit Peace
Element Air – The breath of life that allows the mind to achieve new insights and fresh perspectives, inspiration, active and abstract dreaming, and freedom from attachments.

Degree Choice Points
21° Libra 33'
Light Spontaneous Caring
Shadow Need to be Popular
Wisdom Be receptive to talents that arise from your genetics.

Tenth House Moon
24° Virgo 0'
Tenth House Umbrella Theme
I Relate/I Produce – Your approach to status, career, honor, and prestige, and why you chose your father.
Light Public Recognition
Shadow Separation Anxiety
Wisdom Turn a project over to someone who can complete it.

The Sun is Opposite the Moon

Full moons are always in opposition to the Sun. This creates a feeling of tension between where you want to shine and how your feelings are flowing on a sensory level about the Sun's directive. The two forces seem like they are working against each other, yet they are on the same team displaying different techniques to obtain the same mission. The Libra/Aries polarity creates tension between the idea of "We" versus "Me."

Libra Goddess

Ostara, Goddess of the Spring Equinox, walks into your life creating a carpet of fragrant flowers in her wake with each step upon the Earth. Freed from the ice and snow of Winter, she bathes in the moonlight and breathes out warmer breezes to turn up the temperatures. This moon is the harbinger, a rebirth of the Earth to fresh growth and abundance.

What is blooming new in your life? What do your seeds need to shed and break through to bask in the bright Spring sunlight? Take Ostara's blessing of jasmine or rose fragrance into the bath or shower and allow the warm water to wash away the old.

Build Your Altar

Colors Pink, green
Numerology 4 – Accept loyalty in you relationships
Tarot Card Justice – The ability to stay in the center of polarity
Gemstones Rose quartz, jade
Plant remedy Olive trees – Stamina
Fragrance Eucalyptus – Clarity of breath

Clearing the Slate

Sixty hours before the full moon negative traits connected to the astro-sign might become activated to trigger what needs to be released during the full moon phase. You may notice an unusual need to defend, an over-shadowing guilt, or a need to justify. Make a list of the triggers and do Ho'oponopono, a Hawaiian Huna ritual for forgiveness. Look in the mirror, and for each negative trait, tell yourself *I am sorry, I forgive you, thank you for your awareness,* and *I love you.*

Libra Victories and Challenges

Say all of the statements in this section out loud. Then, underline the phrase that means the most to you. Use the phrase as your special affirmation for recalibrating throughout this phase of the moon.

I am awakened to the reality of the Law of Cause and Effect. I take time out today to see what is coming back to me. I know my actions, my words, and my thoughts have life and manifest in a pattern that returns to me. Today, I am in a place where I can clearly see the results of my words, my actions, and my thoughts. I am aware that it is time for a review and, in so doing, I am given the opportunity to balance, integrate and redistribute these results in a more productive way. When I truly know and experience the Law of Cause and Effect (what I send out comes back to me), I can take responsibility for my actions, words, and thoughts, and set myself free of blame. When blame is gone from my thought pattern (self-inflicted or circumstantial), I am able to benefit from my review rather than wasting energy justifying or defending my position. I now accept the idea that I am free to reconcile with whatever I have labeled as an injustice in my life. I take the time to re-route my thinking towards making life a beneficial experience. Today, I accept that in changing my language I can change my life. Today, I prepare to take actions toward beneficial experiences. Today, I release the need to be right and accept the right to be. Today, I stop judging life and start living life.

Libra Homework

Let the fresh air blow away mental stagnation related to times when you let others' interests supersede your own. Drink an excess amount of water to alert your kidneys that the recalibration process has commenced. It's time to deepen your intention to be one with the light, promoting restoration on Earth.

Recalibrating List

Say this statement out loud three times before writing your recalibrating list:

I am a free spiritual being and it is my desire to be free to think and to express myself fully.

I hereby fully and completely free my mind from all adhesions to outdated philosophies, habits, relationships, groups of people, man-made laws, moral codes, all rules, set ideas and set ways of thinking, traditions, organizations, duty-motivated activities, guilt, judgment, and being misunderstood!

Libra Recalibrating Ideas

Now is the time to activate a game change in my life, and give up situations that are not balanced, people-pleasing and the need to be liked, sorrow over past relationships, unsupportive relationships, the need to be right, false accusations, and being misunderstood.

Activate Acceleration

By acknowledging what you have recalibrated and overcome, you activate your acceleration. Keep this list active during this moon cycle.

Sky Power Yoga

Elevated Legs

You need two bath towels and one to two pillows for the prop.

Nest two towels together. Fold them lengthwise and roll into a log. Place the towel log on the floor and place your pillow on top for your support prop.

Sit on the floor with your legs straight in front of you and your feet hip-width apart.

Place your prop between your feet and then place each foot on the prop.

Sit up straight. Lower yourself onto your elbows and then onto your back. Relax. Close your

eyes. Breathe in and out slowly and deeply several times through your nose with your awareness on your kidneys.

Inhale deeply. Say the mantra *I Relate* either out loud or in your head. Exhale slowly. Enjoy breathing with your mantra for a few minutes in this relaxing and rejuvenating pose.

Full Moon in Libra

How to Use the Moon Book With Your Chart

Fill in the blanks on the Cosmic Check-In page. Then look up the degree of the Moon on the chart below. Take note of the "I" statement on the outside of the wheel where the Moon is located. Now, locate the same degree on your own chart and make a note of the house and corresponding

"I" statement. Go back to the Cosmic Check-In page and circle the two statements from the charts and read what you wrote. This will give you an idea about what to expect from this moon phase on a personal level.

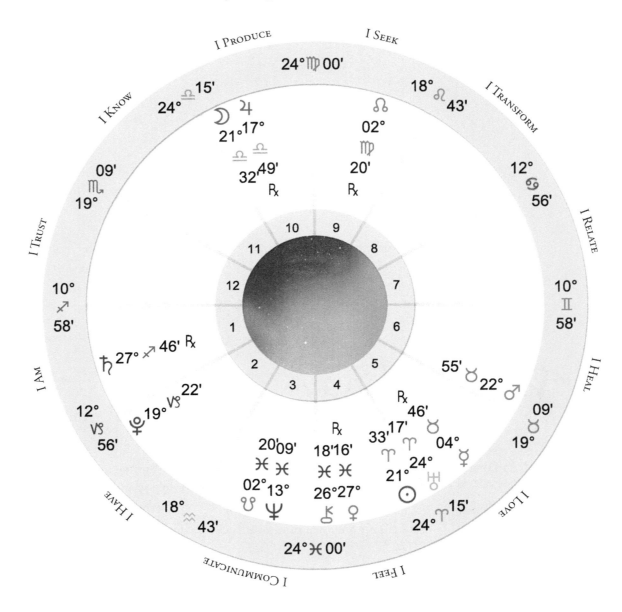

♈	Aries	♋ Cancer	♐ Sagittarius	☽ Moon	♄ Saturn	☊ North Node	V/C Void-of-Course
♉	Taurus	♌ Leo	♑ Capricorn	☿ Mercury	♅ Uranus	☋ South Node	▲ Super-Sensitivity
♊	Gemini	♍ Virgo	♒ Aquarius	♀ Venus	♆ Neptune	➡ Enters	▼ Low-Vitality
		♎ Libra	♓ Pisces	♂ Mars	♇ Pluto	℞ Retrograde	
		♏ Scorpio	☉ Sun	♃ Jupiter	⚷ Chiron	S/D Stationary Direct	

Cosmic Check-in

Take a moment to write a brief phrase for each "I" statement. This activates all areas of your life for this creative cycle.

♎ I Relate

♏ I Transform

♐ I Seek

♑ I Produce

♒ I Know

♓ I Trust

♈ I Am

♉ I Have

♊ I Communicate

♋ I Feel

♌ I Love

♍ I Heal

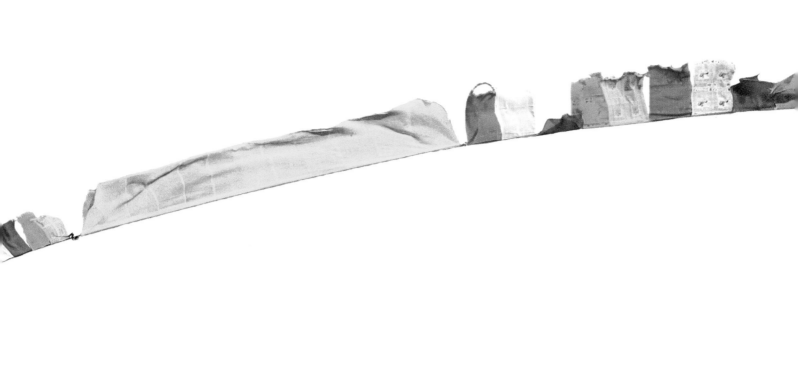

New Moon in Taurus

April 26th, 5:16 AM

Statement I Have
Body Neck
Mind Collector
Spirit Accumulation
Element Earth – Acquisition, create abundance, increase abundance, and practice generosity.

Degree Choice Points
6° Taurus 27'
Light Awakening
Shadow Shaming
Wisdom Walk in nature to relieve fear.

First House Moon
17° Aries 15'

First House Umbrella Theme
I Am/I Have – Your outer appearance, the way you present yourself, the way you dress, the way you enter a room, and what you leave behind when you leave the room.
Light Respite
Shadow Workaholic
Wisdom Use fluorite to focus your mind.

When the Sun is in Taurus

Taurus is the time when we see the true manifesting power, as the plants move to a higher aspiration of life and bloom. Once again, we become connected to the essence of beauty as a symbol of our divinity. Taurus is the connection between humanity and divinity. Taurus' job is to infuse matter with light through accumulating layers of substance. This is why they are such good shoppers and collectors. The more they accumulate, the more divinity they experience. This process brings about a sense of self-value which is directly commensurate to the amount of money they manifest. Personal resources are part of the pattern. Discover your value at this time.

Taurus Goddess

Today, Lakshmi, the Hindu Goddess of Abundance, walks into your life bearing gifts. She joyously showers you with success, wealth, well-being, luck, happiness, and fulfillment. Her blessings also include forgiveness and the generosity of spirit that allows you to reap the recognition for good work well done.

Working with feng shui, place a statue of Lakshmi in the left-hand corner of your room (looking in from the entrance) to honor her and to signal your receptivity. Are your hands and heart open and ready to receive? Make space for the new. Step confidently into the flow of abundance! Take Lakshmi's lead and shower everyone you meet with kindness and generosity!

Build Your Altar

Colors Green, pink, deep red, earth tones
Numerology 2 – Balance occurs with loving service
Tarot Card Hierophant – The ability to listen, inner-knowing
Gemstones Topaz, agate, smoky quartz, jade, rose quartz
Plant Remedy Angelica – Connecting Heaven and Earth
Fragrance Rose – Opening the heart

Taurus Victories and Challenges

Say all of the statements in this section out loud. Then, underline the phrase that means the most to you. Use the phrase as your special affirmation for manifesting throughout this phase of the moon.

Everything is possible for me today. My possibilities are endless. I have the power within me to make all of my dreams come true. I have the tools to make my talent a reality. I have the power to identify with my talent. Today, I focus my attention and intention on manifesting with my talent and, in so doing, I transform my ideas into reality. I recognize the part of me that is connected to the cosmic source of ideas and I express that source within me to manifest my creative power. I see my possibilities and act on them today. I am the creative power. I am all-knowing. I am an individual. There is no one else like me. I can manifest anything I desire. I intend it, I allow it, so be it.

Rules for Manifesting

Know what you want. Write it down. Say it out loud. Recognize that because you thought it, it can be so. Release your limiting beliefs. Override your limiting beliefs with power statements. Act as if you have already manifested your idea. Lastly, value yourself!

Taurus Homework

Taureans manifest best when buying, selling, and owning real estate, gardening and landscaping, selling and collecting art, manufacturing and selling fine furniture, singing or acting, and as a restaurateur, antique dealer, or interior designer.

The Taurus moon asks us to infuse light into form and, in so doing, the bridge between humanity and divinity is actualized and we can assume our stewardship in the physical world. When we release Spirit into matter, we become open to the idea that accumulation and actualization set us free to experience the abundance available to us here on Earth. Go shopping!

Manifesting List

This or something better than this comes to me in an easy and pleasurable way, for the good of all concerned. Thank you, Universe!

Taurus Manifesting Ideas

Now is the time to focus on manifesting success, money, property, luxury, beauty, personal value, and pleasure.

Gratitude List

Keep this list active throughout the moon cycle. This will bring you to a level of completion so that a new cycle of opportunity can occur in your life. Be prepared for miracles!

Sky Power Yoga

Seated Neck Rolls

You need one chair for the prop.

Sit one hand-width forward from the back of the chair. Back is straight and feet are placed hip-width apart on the floor. If your feet require more solid contact with the floor, place pillows or folded towels under your feet.

Relax and close your eyes. Breathe in and out slowly and deeply several times through your nose, with your awareness on your throat.

As you exhale, drop your head forward rolling the right ear toward the right shoulder.

Inhale and tip your chin up slightly while you envision the energy of your breath coming into your neck. Say or think to yourself the mantra *I Have*.

Exhale softly and slowly as you roll your head forward and to the opposite direction with the left ear towards the left shoulder.

Inhale, tipping your chin slightly up and repeating the mantra, then exhale rolling back toward the right shoulder. Repeat as desired.

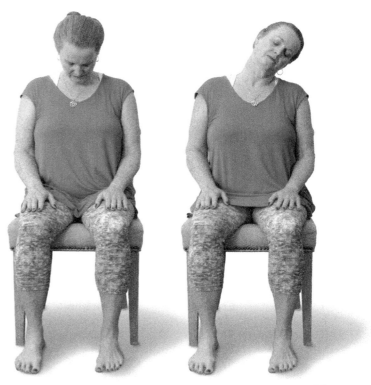

81

New Moon in Taurus

How to Use the Moon Book With Your Chart

Fill in the blanks on the Cosmic Check-In page. Then look up the degree of the Moon on the chart below. Take note of the "I" statement on the outside of the wheel where the Moon is located. Now, locate the same degree on your own chart and make a note of the house and corresponding

"I" statement. Go back to the Cosmic Check-In page and circle the two statements from the charts and read what you wrote. This will give you an idea about what to expect from this moon phase on a personal level.

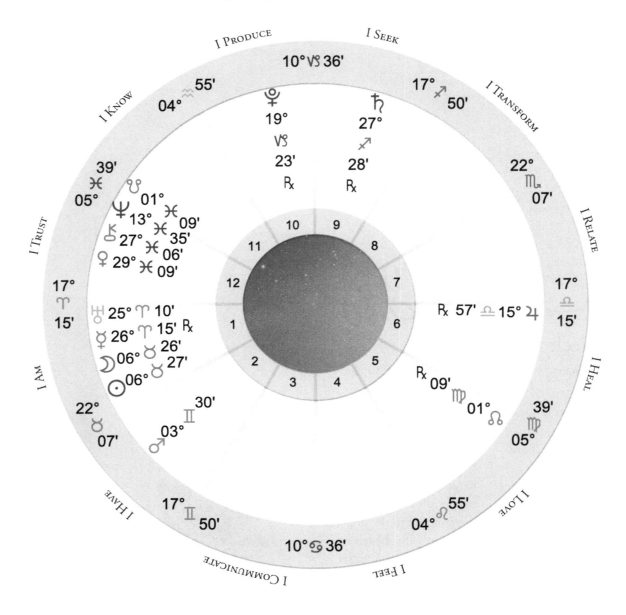

♈ Aries	♋ Cancer	♐ Sagittarius
♉ Taurus	♌ Leo	♑ Capricorn
♊ Gemini	♍ Virgo	♒ Aquarius
	♎ Libra	♓ Pisces
	♏ Scorpio	☉ Sun

☽ Moon	♄ Saturn	☊ North Node
☿ Mercury	♅ Uranus	☋ South Node
♀ Venus	♆ Neptune	➡ Enters
♂ Mars	♇ Pluto	℞ Retrograde
♃ Jupiter	⚷ Chiron	S/D Stationary Direct

V/C Void-of-Course
▲ Super-Sensitivity
▼ Low-Vitality

82

Cosmic Check-in

Take a moment to write a brief phrase for each "I" statement. This activates all areas of your life for this creative cycle.

♉ I Have

♊ I Communicate

♋ I Feel

♌ I Love

♍ I Heal

♎ I Relate

♏ I Transform

♐ I Seek

♑ I Produce

♒ I Know

♓ I Trust

♈ I Am

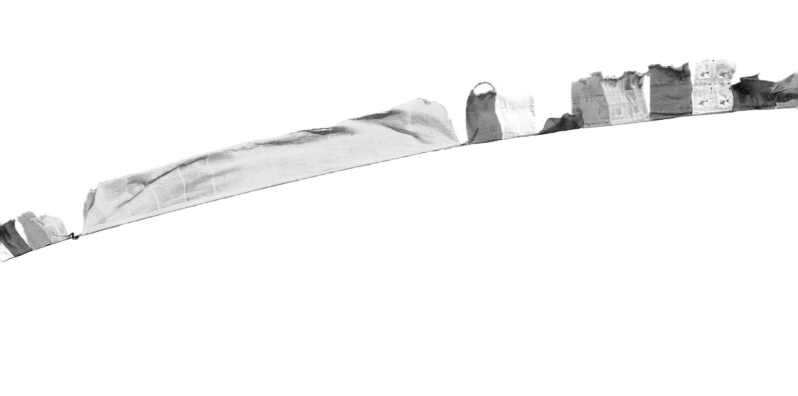

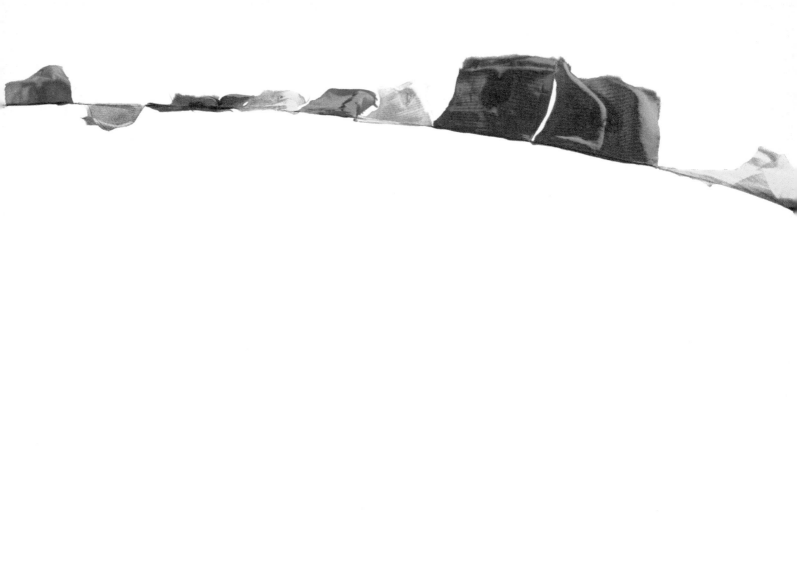

May

Planetary Highlights

Until June 9: Jupiter retrograde in Libra

Acknowledge the benefits of your relationships. Share gratitude with those you love.

Until August 25: Saturn retrograde in Sagittarius

How does *less is more* apply to your life?

Until September 28: Pluto retrograde in Capricorn

How do you want to expand your wealth? Stick to your plan to create abundance.

Until November 22: Neptune retrograde in Pisces

If you realize your dream was an illusion, face your sadness. Recognize what didn't come true, recalibrate yourself, and create a new practical approach to realize your dreams.

May 3: Mercury direct in Aries

How would you ideally like to represent yourself, your business, or an important project? Now is the time to run with your optimal ideas.

May 9: Retrograde North Node in Leo

This switch is a game changer. Refocus your goals related to love, to creativity, to risk, to glamour and to fun. Go for it! Flow with these energies and know your destination will be better than before.

May 10-27: Mercury and Uranus coupled in Aries

A major acceleration—new ideas bring new beginnings. Focus on freedom, truth, and innovation.

May 13-14: Super Sensitivity

Slow down to avoid getting carried away by the winds of too much mental activity.

May 15: Mercury enters Taurus

Let your ideas become reality.

May 20: Sun enters Gemini

Shine and get your message out!

May 23-28: Retrograde Jupiter in Libra opposite Uranus in Aries

Good fortune and new beginnings are playing on the same team. Integrate—don't separate.

May 27-28: Low Vitality

Stay safe and close to home as earth changes are possible.

Sunday	Monday	Tuesday	Wednesday	Thursday	Friday	Saturday
	1 ☿♃♄♇℞ ☽V/C 1:22 PM ☽→♌ 9:11 PM 7. Your conscience leads to insight.	**2** ☿♃♄♇℞ 8. Make the law of sound work for you.	**3** ♃♄♇℞ ☽V/C 9:35 PM ☋—9:34AM 24°♈15′ 9. Find compassion in your heart.	**4** ♃♄♇℞ ☽→♍ 2:46 AM 10. Let acceleration provide the answer.	**5** ♃♄♇℞ 2. Touch the body to help stabilize it.	**6** ♃♄♇℞ ☽V/C 5:42 AM ☽→♎ 11:20 AM 3. Use color as a language to create.
7 ♃♄♇℞ 4. See yourself being better each day.	**8** ♃♄♇℞ ☽V/C 3:58 PM ☽→♏ 10:00 PM 5. Every experience is an opportunity.	**9** ♃♄♇℞ ☊℞→♌ 11:08AM 6. Simplify, keep love in your heart.	**10** ♃♄♇℞ ○20°♏24′2:42PM ☽V/C 2:42 PM 7. Using thought is more effective today.	**11** ♃♄♇℞ ☽→♐ 9:59 AM 8. Stay ready and open with grace.	**12** ♃♄♇℞ 9. Love is the energy of oneness.	**13** ♃♄♇℞▲ ☽V/C 7:14 PM ☽→♑ 10:37 PM 10. Flow with what is in front of you.
14 ♃♄♇℞▲ Mother's Day 2. Only in the present is there peace.	**15** ♃♄♇℞ ♀→♉ 9:08PM 3. Let the child within play today.	**16** ♃♄♇℞ ☽V/C 3:22 AM ☽→♒ 10:49 AM 4. Focus on structures that work.	**17** ♃♄♇℞ 5. Everything you do affects the world.	**18** ♃♄♇℞ ☽V/C 5:32 PM ☽→♓ 8:51 PM 6. The core of community is unity.	**19** ♃♄♇℞ 7. Walk in the dignity of your truth.	**20** ♃♄♇℞ ☽V/C 8:39 PM ☉→♊ 1:32 PM 8. You manifest from your knowing.
21 ♃♄♇℞ ☽→♈ 3:10 AM 9. Choose happiness it's the best choice.	**22** ♃♄♇℞ ☽V/C 11:59 PM 10. When it's over, move on.	**23** ♃♄♇℞ ☽→♉ 5:32 AM 11. You are a universal light being.	**24** ♃♄♇℞ ☽V/C 12:08 PM 3. Imagination is the source of creation.	**25** ♃♄♇℞ ●4°♊47′12:44PM ☽→♊ 5:15 AM 4. Stay organized and plans work.	**26** ♃♄♇℞ ☽V/C 11:18 PM 5. Even the truth is constantly changing.	**27** ♃♄♇℞▼ ☽→♋ 4:24 AM 7. If you can think it, you can do it.
28 ♃♄♇℞▼ ☽V/C 11:58 PM 8. Celebrate the success of others.	**29** ♃♄♇℞ Memorial Day ☽→♌ 5:11 AM 9. Call on your angels for help.	**30** ♃♄♇℞ 10. Make room for something new.	**31** ♃♄♇℞ ☽V/C 4:14 AM ☽→♍ 9:15 AM 2. Balance brings wellbeing.			

♈ Aries	♎ Libra	☉ Sun	♄ Saturn	☊ North Node	▲ Super Sensitivity	6. Love
♉ Taurus	♏ Scorpio	☽ Moon	♅ Uranus	☋ South Node	▼ Low Vitality	7. Learning
♊ Gemini	♐ Sagittarius	☿ Mercury	♆ Neptune	➡ Enters	2. Balance	8. Money
♋ Cancer	♑ Capricorn	♀ Venus	♇ Pluto	℞ Retrograde	3. Fun	9. Spirituality
♌ Leo	♒ Aquarius	♂ Mars	⚷ Chiron	S/D Stationary Direct	4. Structure	10. Visionary
♍ Virgo	♓ Pisces	♃ Jupiter		V/C Void-of-Course	5. Action	11. Completion

Full Moon in Scorpio

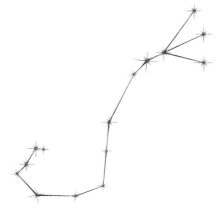

May 10th, 2:42 PM

Statement I Transform

Body Reproductive Organs

Mind Intensity

Spirit Transformation

Element Water – Naturally flows to the lowest ground, consuming emotions, need to nourish the soul, and sensitivity to others.

Degree Choice Points
20° Scorpio 24'

Light Conscientious Objection

Shadow Anarchy

Wisdom Be true to yourself through genuine self-expression.

Third House Moon
16° Scorpio 0'

Third House Umbrella Theme
I Communicate/I Transform – How you get the word out and the message behind your words.

Light Creating Reality

Shadow Over-responsible

Wisdom Your reality comes from your imagination and imagery from all your lifetimes.

The Sun is Opposite the Moon

Full moons are always in opposition to the Sun. This creates a feeling of tension between where you want to shine and how your feelings are flowing on a sensory level about the Sun's directive. The two forces seem like they are working against each other, yet they are on the same team displaying different techniques to obtain the same mission. The Scorpio/Taurus polarity creates tension between sharing resources and living abundantly for yourself.

Scorpio Goddess

The concept of web thinking, in which all is intrinsically interconnected and related to the whole, comes to us through the creator myths of the Pueblo and Hopi people, as Grandmother Spider. She spun a sparkling dew-dropped web and threw it up into the night sky to create the stars.

Her interdependent web of light reminds us to promote the power of community and band together to take action when important issues affect the whole. Grandmother Spider can help you appreciate your own and others' unique contributions and talents, and show you how to combine them to create a strong and sustainable web of action.

Build Your Altar

Colors Indigo, deep purple, scarlet

Numerology 7 – Using thought is more effective than thinking.

Tarot Card Death – The ability to make changes

Gemstones Topaz, tanzanite, onyx, obsidian

Plant remedy Manzanita – Prepares the body for transformation

Fragrance Sandalwood – Awakens your sensuality

Clearing the Slate

Sixty hours before the full moon negative traits connected to the astro-sign might become activated to trigger what needs to be released during the full moon phase. You may notice a deep desire to be secretive, resist sharing money, a feeling of revenge, or the need to create control dramas.

Make a list of the triggers and do Ho'oponopono, a Hawaiian Huna ritual for forgiveness. Look in the mirror, and for each negative trait, tell yourself *I am sorry, I forgive you, thank you for your awareness,* and *I love you.*

Scorpio Victories and Challenges

Say all of the statements in this section out loud. Then, underline the phrase that means the most to you. Use the phrase as your special affirmation for recalibrating throughout this phase of the moon.

I will not compromise myself today. I know that transformation occurs when I stand tall in my truth, even if everything around me needs to die. I see death as a new beginning and know that in death comes new aliveness. I am willing to embrace transformation and open to the idea that change is in my favor. I know that in letting go, I give new life to myself. I am willing to accept that life is ever-changing and in a constant state of renewal; one cannot occur without the other.

Releasing is easy when I offer myself something new. When I allow for the motion of change to stay alive, I let go with one hand and receive with the other hand. The ever-present flow and motion keeps me alive and connected to the revitalizing power of Nature. When the power of Nature becomes apparent to me, I become aware that Nature abhors a vacuum. Rejuvenation is mine when I embrace change.

Scorpio Homework

The Scorpio moon creates the urge within us to make life happen. Pay attention to these urges so you can prepare yourself for greater action, intention, and purpose.

Recalibrating List

Say this statement out loud three times before writing your recalibrating list:

I am a free spiritual being and it is my desire to be free to think and to express myself fully.

I am now free and ready to make choices beyond survival!

Scorpio Recalibrating Ideas

Now is the time to activate a game change in my life, and give up resentment, jealousy, revenge, vendettas, betrayals, blocks to transformation, destructive relationships, unhealthy joint financial situations, obstacles to having a healthy sex life, resistance to changing paradigms, and karma relating to all issues of power.

Activate Acceleration

By acknowledging what you have recalibrated and overcome, you activate your acceleration. Keep this list active during this moon cycle.

Sky Power Yoga

Reclined Goddess on a Chair

You need one chair for the prop.

Sit on the floor close to your chair with the right side of your upper torso facing the chair seat and your lower torso close to the chair legs.

Lean back onto your left elbow and lift your right leg onto the chair seat. With your back flat on the floor, lift your left leg to rest on the chair seat next to the right leg.

Place the bottoms of your feet together in the center of the chair seat. Allow your knees to fall towards the edges of the chair seat. Adjust your knees to allow your thighs to open comfortably.

Relax. Close your eyes. Breathe in and out slowly and deeply several times through your nose with your awareness on your reproductive organs.

Inhale deeply as you say or think to yourself the mantra *I Transform.*

Exhale slowly and relax into the pose more deeply with each out breath. Repeat as desired.

91

Full Moon in Scorpio

How to Use the Moon Book With Your Chart

Fill in the blanks on the Cosmic Check-In page. Then look up the degree of the Moon on the chart below. Take note of the "I" statement on the outside of the wheel where the Moon is located. Now, locate the same degree on your own chart and make a note of the house and corresponding

"I" statement. Go back to the Cosmic Check-In page and circle the two statements from the charts and read what you wrote. This will give you an idea about what to expect from this moon phase on a personal level.

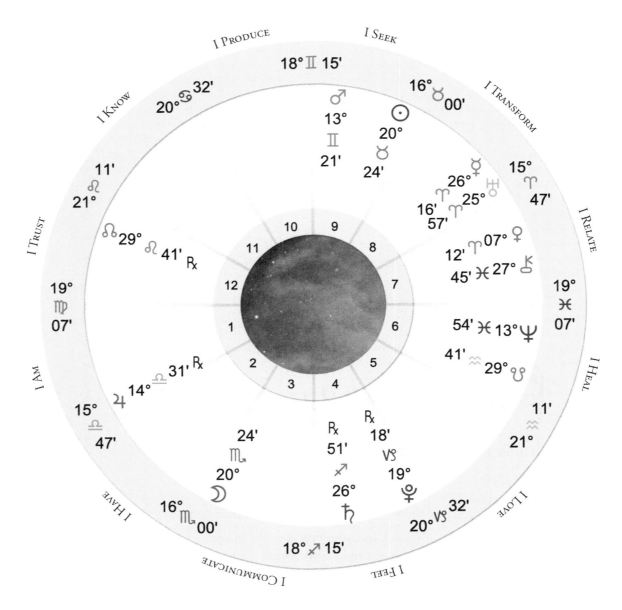

♈ Aries	♋ Cancer	♐ Sagittarius	☽ Moon	♄ Saturn	☊ North Node	V/C Void-of-Course
♉ Taurus	♌ Leo	♑ Capricorn	☿ Mercury	♅ Uranus	☋ South Node	▲ Super-Sensitivity
♊ Gemini	♍ Virgo	♒ Aquarius	♀ Venus	♆ Neptune	➡ Enters	▼ Low-Vitality
	♎ Libra	♓ Pisces	♂ Mars	♇ Pluto	℞ Retrograde	
	♏ Scorpio	☉ Sun	♃ Jupiter	⚷ Chiron	♗/♙ Stationary Direct	

Cosmic Check-in

Take a moment to write a brief phrase for each "I" statement. This activates all areas of your life for this creative cycle.

♏ I Transform

♐ I Seek

♑ I Produce

♒ I Know

♓ I Trust

♈ I Am

♉ I Have

♊ I Communicate

♋ I Feel

♌ I Love

♍ I Heal

♎ I Relate

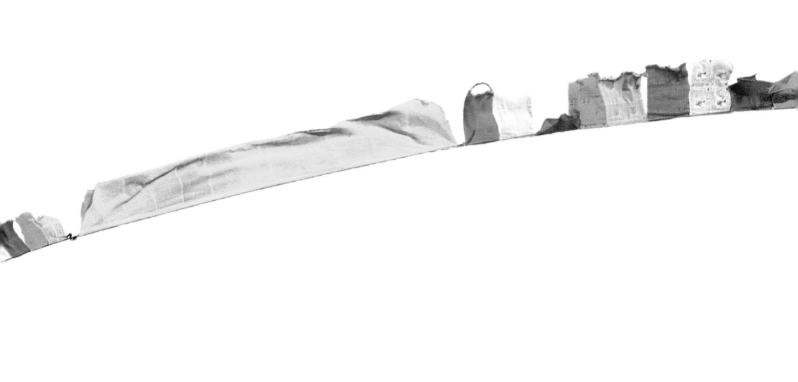

New Moon in Gemini

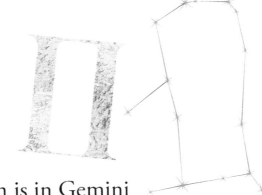

May 25th, 12:44 PM

Statement I Communicate

Body Lungs and Hands

Mind Intellect

Spirit Intelligence

Element Air – Freedom from attachment, curiosity, flexibility, the breath of life that gives new insights and fresh perspectives, and active and abstract dreaming.

Degree Choice Points
4° Gemini 47'

Light Social Reform

Shadow Contradictions

Wisdom Communicate your visions in a balanced way.

Tenth House Moon
4° Gemini 24'

Tenth House Umbrella Theme
I Produce/I Communicate – Your approach to status, career, honor, and prestige, and why you chose your father.

Light Social Reform

Shadow Contradictions

Wisdom Communicate your visions in a balanced way.

When the Sun is in Gemini

This is a time when the ability to communicate is at the top of the priority list. Allow your thoughts to lead you to a formula for success so you can put your thoughts into action. Then, find the appropriate soapbox to stand on so your message can be heard. Right now is the time to make your message clear, enlightening, witty, and thought-provoking. Your bright mind is at its high throne and waiting for an audience. Try blogging, do a show on YouTube, join Toastmasters, write that screenplay, film yourself doing a travel show, start a discussion group, or write a newsletter for your neighborhood. Most of all, put your bright mind to work!

Gemini Goddess

Some of Zeus's favorite consorts were the nymphs who lived on Mount Kithairon. One in particular, Echo, incurred Zeus' wife Hera's wrath. As punishment for trying to protect Zeus, Hera cursed Echo with only being able to speak the last few words spoken to her. In love with Narcissus, Echo was unable to speak her own truth, and watched as Narcissus fell in love with himself, abetted by the words he spoke that Echo was forced to repeat back to him. After he died, Echo physically wasted away, leaving only the sound of her voice.

During this Gemini full moon, attend to your communications! Be curious about what ripples your speech and writing may generate. What reverberates and repeats? Is it your truth?

Build Your Altar

Colors Bright yellow, orange, multi-colors

Numerology 4 – Stay organized and know your plan works

Tarot Card Lovers – Connecting to wholeness

Gemstones Yellow diamond, citrine

Plant Remedy Morning Glory – Thinking with your heart not your head

Fragrance Iris – The ability to focus the mind

Gemini Victories *and* Challenges

Say all of the statements in this section out loud. Then, underline the phrase that means the most to you. Use the phrase as your special affirmation for manifesting throughout this phase of the moon.

I am dark. I am light. I am day. I am night. The extremes in life exist within me, completing themselves in reality. The "I" that is "we" lives within me. I am one in the same. I am both.

I know that flow comes from accepting my opposite natures. Today, I accept my opposites and get into the flow. I am aware today of how my judgments separate me from people, events, experiences, and, most of all, from myself. Today, I am going to see where I have separated all of the parts of myself and begin to integrate into wholeness through acceptance and understanding. I begin by breathing. I breathe in wholeness and breathe out separation. I understand that breath is life and that life includes all facets of my experience to gain awareness. I know that I am Heaven. I know that I am Earth. I know that I am masculine. I know that I am feminine. Today, I become unified. Today, I integrate into wholeness. I breathe into all of these aspects of myself, knowing that in my totality I am connected to Oneness. The "I" that is "we" lives within me. I am one in the same. I am both.

Gemini Homework

Geminis manifest best through broadcasting and journalism, as a speech coach, comedian, political satirist, gossip columnist, negotiator, media specialist, manicurist, salesperson, teacher, or travel consultant.

Expect to awaken your will on seven levels…

- The will to direct – through the power of your original intention.

- The will to love – stimulating goodwill among humankind through cooperation.

- The will to act – by laying foundations for a happier world.

- The will to cooperate – the desire and demand for right relationships.

- The will to know – to think correctly and creatively so that every man/woman can find their outstanding characteristics.

- The will to persist – to be one with your light and represent the ideal standard for living.

- The will to organize – to carry forward direct inspiration through groups of goodwill.

Manifesting List

This or something better than this comes to me in an easy and pleasurable way, for the good of all concerned. Thank you, Universe!

Gemini Manifesting Ideas

Now is the time to focus on manifesting communications, a promotion, technology, ideas, non-judgmental communication, thinking outside of duality, a quiet mind, charisma and charm, and flirting.

Gratitude List

Keep this list active throughout the moon cycle. This will bring you to a level of completion so that a new cycle of opportunity can occur in your life. Be prepared for miracles!

Sky Power Yoga

Seated Camel

You need one chair for the prop.

Sit one hand-width forward from the back of the chair. Your back is straight and your feet are placed hip-width apart on the floor.

Lengthen the spine and slightly tuck your chin. Then interlace your fingers behind your back with your knuckles facing down.

Relax. Close your eyes. Breathe in and out slowly and deeply several times through your nose with your awareness on your lungs and hands.

Inhale deeply. Lift your chest and press your hands down and backwards. Say or think to yourself the mantra *I Communicate*.

Exhale slowly. Release the pose by bending your elbows and dropping your chest back to normal.
Repeat as desired.

New Moon in Gemini

How to Use the Moon Book With Your Chart

Fill in the blanks on the Cosmic Check-In page. Then look up the degree of the Moon on the chart below. Take note of the "I" statement on the outside of the wheel where the Moon is located. Now, locate the same degree on your own chart and make a note of the house and corresponding

"I" statement. Go back to the Cosmic Check-In page and circle the two statements from the charts and read what you wrote. This will give you an idea about what to expect from this moon phase on a personal level.

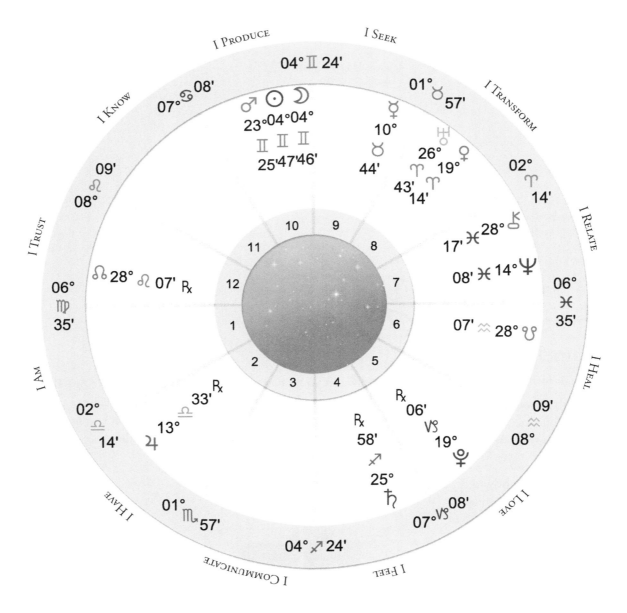

♈	Aries	♋	Cancer	♐	Sagittarius	☽ Moon	♄ Saturn	☊ North Node	V/C Void-of-Course
♉	Taurus	♌	Leo	♑	Capricorn	☿ Mercury	♅ Uranus	☋ South Node	▲ Super-Sensitivity
♊	Gemini	♍	Virgo	♒	Aquarius	♀ Venus	♆ Neptune	➡ Enters	▼ Low-Vitality
		♎	Libra	♓	Pisces	♂ Mars	♇ Pluto	℞ Retrograde	
		♏	Scorpio	☉	Sun	♃ Jupiter	⚷ Chiron	S/D Stationary Direct	

Cosmic Check-in

Take a moment to write a brief phrase for each "I" statement. This activates all areas of your life for this creative cycle.

Ⅱ I Communicate

♋ I Feel

♌ I Love

♍ I Heal

♎ I Relate

♏ I Transform

♐ I Seek

♑ I Produce

♒ I Know

♓ I Trust

♈ I Am

♉ I Have

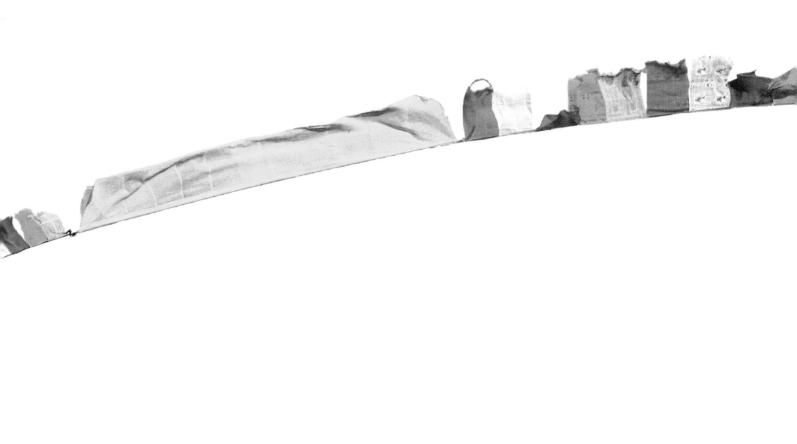

June

Planetary Highlights

Until June 9: Jupiter retrograde in Libra

Acknowledge the fortunate gifts of your friends by treasuring your heart-centered relationships. Review relationships from 2005. Update or release with love any unbalanced relationships.

Until August 25: Saturn retrograde in Sagittarius

What needs to be refined? Sagittarius energy can miss important details, so check in to refine and move on. Does your family need healing? Connect with grace, ease, and freedom to bring much-needed joy into your family life.

Until September 28: Pluto retrograde in Capricorn

Pluto, the great transformer, asks what demands to be transformed? If you have a tendency to hold on, go for a bigger picture. You won't have regrets if you let go and surrender to Pluto's transformational power.

June 3-5: Low Vitality

Don't resist it if you feel exhausted. Earth changes are possible so stay close to home and get rest.

June 4: Mars enters Cancer

Your feelings sizzle when this ball of fire lands in the ocean of existence. Be aware that what you have been storing—or hiding—may emerge. Watch your flashbacks, make new choices.

June 6: Mercury enters Gemini

Let your mind shine! Get your message out via inspiring conversations and marketing communications that get you the attention you deserve.

June 6: Venus enters Taurus

Go shopping and enjoy luxury. Have fun, go dancing, go to a concert, make love—do whatever makes you happy.

June 9: Jupiter direct in Libra

Set yourself free as you celebrate the completion of your review of 2005.

June 10-11: Super Sensitivity

Don't rush! An inability to focus your mind could make you prone to accidents. Stay safe.

June 16-November 22: Neptune retrograde in Pisces

Is your life on hold due to unfulfilled promises? Advance beyond them so greater freedom manifests.

June 20: Summer Solstice—Sun enters Cancer

Celebrate light and the lightness of being! Look at your garden of dreams, what needs your attention this summer?

June 20-21: Low Vitality

Don't resist it if you feel exhausted. Earth changes are possible so stay close to home and get rest.

June 23: Pluto opposite Mars

The ego is up for a test! Where do you need to be right? Expect power trips where change is needed related to money. Resolve your money karma and avoid starting a hostile battle, if possible.

June 30-December 4: Chiron retrograde in Pisces

Reach out to heal. Don't let a tendency towards isolation fool you into thinking you will heal faster alone.

Sunday	Monday	Tuesday	Wednesday	Thursday	Friday	Saturday
				1 ♃♄♇℞ 3. God within is the source of creation.	2 ♃♄♇℞ ☽V/C 2:48 PM ☽→♎ 5:03 PM 4. Cooperation is a natural condition.	3 ♃♄♇℞ ▼ 5. Pay attention to what you see.
4 ♃♄♇℞ ▼ ♂→♋ 9:17AM 6. Love accelerates and amplifies joy.	5 ♃♄♇℞ ▼ ☽V/C 1:56 AM ☽→♏ 3:45 AM 7. Be your own teacher first.	6 ♃♄♇℞ ☽V/C 5:35 PM ☿→♊ 3:16 PM ♀→♉ 12:28 AM 8. Add money to your creative power.	7 ♃♄♇℞ ☽→♐ 3:59 PM 9. Give this day all that is Divine.	8 ♃♄♇℞ 10. Transcend the hurt in your life.	9 ♄♇℞ ○ 18°♐53′ 6:09AM ☽V/C 11:20 PM ♃S/D 7:04 AM 13°♎13′ 2. Look ahead, yesterday is gone.	10 ♄♇℞ ▲ ☽→♑ 4:36 AM 3. Find fulfillment in being social.
11 ♄♇℞ ▲ 4. Accelerate your plans.	12 ♄♇℞ ☽V/C 11:45AM ☽→♒ 4:44PM 5. Do things you have put off.	13 ♄♇℞ 6. You are living proof love exists.	14 ♄♇℞ Flag Day ☽V/C 10:39PM 7. Let your mind breathe today.	15 ♄♇℞ ☽→♓ 3:17AM 8. There will always be more to enjoy.	16 ♄♆♇℞ ♆℞ 14°♓15′ - 4:11AM 9. Prayer is Spirit manifesting.	17 ♄♆♇℞ ☽V/C 4:32 AM ☽→♈ 10:54AM 10. Your future depends on you.
18 ♄♆♇℞ Father's Day 2. Balance occurs with breath.	19 ♄♆♇℞ ☽V/C 12:42 PM ☽→♉ 2:52 PM 3. A playful attitude enriches your spirit.	20 ♄♆♇℞ ▼ ☽V/C 9:25 PM Summer Solstice ☉→♋ 9:25 PM 4. Teamwork celebrates synergy.	21 ♄♆♇℞ ▼ ☽→♊ 3:44 PM ☿→♋ 2:59 AM 5. When in doubt, make a change.	22 ♄♆♇℞ 6. Flowers make your heart happy.	23 ♄♆♇℞ ▼ ● 2°♋47′ 7:30PM ☽V/C 11:45 AM ☽→♋ 3:06 PM 7. All events in our lives teach us.	24 ♄♆♇℞ ▼ 8. Manifest your truth today.
25 ♄♆♇℞ ☽V/C 11:44 AM ☽→♌ 3:06 PM 9. Forgive yourself.	26 ♄♆♇℞ 10. Trust what you know.	27 ♄♆♇℞ ☽V/C 2:11 PM ☽→♍ 5:41 PM 2. Stress arises when the mind resists.	28 ♄♆♇℞ 3. All creation takes place in the heart.	29 ♄♆♇℞ ☽V/C 1:34 PM 4. Control doesn't equal happiness.	30 ♄♆⚷♇℞ ☽→♎ 12:01 AM ⚷S℞ 28°♓51′ - 12:09AM 5. Your strength is your vitality.	

♈ Aries
♉ Taurus
♊ Gemini
♋ Cancer
♌ Leo
♍ Virgo
♎ Libra
♏ Scorpio
♐ Sagittarius
♑ Capricorn
♒ Aquarius
♓ Pisces
☉ Sun
☽ Moon
☿ Mercury
♀ Venus
♂ Mars
♃ Jupiter
♄ Saturn
♅ Uranus
♆ Neptune
♇ Pluto
⚷ Chiron
☊ North Node
☋ South Node
→ Enters
℞ Retrograde
S/D Stationary Direct
V/C Void-of-Course
▲ Super Sensitivity
▼ Low Vitality
2. Balance
3. Fun
4. Structure
5. Action
6. Love
7. Learning
8. Money
9. Spirituality
10. Visionary
11. Completion

Full Moon in Sagittarius

June 9th, 6:09 AM

Statement I Seek
Body Thighs
Mind Culture
Spirit Higher Knowledge
Element Fire – The ability to stand up for yourself, inspiration, cleansing, passion, and optimism.

Degree Choice Points
18° Sagittarius 53'
Light Migration
Shadow Unhealthy Habitat
Wisdom Communicate directly with your internal source.

Sixth House Moon
16° Scorpio 20'
Sixth House Umbrella Theme
I Heal/I Transform – The way you manage your body and appearance. Family lineage and DNA healing, knowing abundance, healing power from the plant kingdom and nutrition, body awareness, and connection to small animals.
Light Creating Reality
Shadow Over-responsible
Wisdom Your reality comes from your imagination and imagery from all your lifetimes.

The Sun is Opposite the Moon

Full moons are always in opposition to the Sun. This creates a feeling of tension between where you want to shine and how your feelings are flowing on a sensory level about the Sun's directive.

The two forces seem like they are working against each other, yet they are on the same team displaying different techniques to obtain the same mission. The Sagittarius/Gemini polarity creates tension between the quest for higher knowledge and the need for academic accolades.

Sagittarius Goddess

Pythia was the title bestowed upon the priestess who channeled the Oracle of Delphi at the Temple of Apollo. The rambling prophecies she spoke were induced by breathing the vapors rising out of the chasm in the rocks, at a site formerly dedicated to the great Earth Goddess, Gaia.

Allow yourself quiet meditation time with your favorite divination tool (Tarot cards, pendulum, automatic writing) and give yourself over to messages you receive. Remember that Pythia calls forth her art through the magic of breathwork, which operates without hallucinogenic vapors! Seek the messages she delivers from the wisdom and stored history of the Earth. Find a rock to sit on and breathe!

Build Your Altar

Colors Deep purple, turquoise, royal blue
Numerology 2 – Remember that yesterday is gone
Tarot Card Temperance – Balancing the present with the past, updating yourself
Gemstone Turquoise
Plant remedy Madia – Seeing and hitting the target
Fragrance Magnolia – Expanded beauty

Clearing the Slate

June 9th
6:09 AM

Sixty hours before the full moon negative traits connected to the astro-sign might become activated to trigger what needs to be released during the full moon phase. You may notice a sudden urge to be excessive, to resist reality by exaggerating, to speak before thinking, to be blunt, or to use unfiltered language. Make a list of the triggers and do Ho'oponopono, a Hawaiian Huna ritual for forgiveness. Look in the mirror, and for each negative trait, tell yourself *I am sorry, I forgive you, thank you for your awareness,* and *I love you.*

Sagittarius Victories and Challenges

Say all of the statements in this section out loud. Then, underline the phrase that means the most to you. Use the phrase as your special affirmation for recalibrating throughout this phase of the moon.

Today, I blend my old self with my new self, my physical reality with my spiritual awareness, my positive thoughts with my negative thoughts, my past with my present, my feminine with my masculine, my rewards with my losses, my ups with my downs, and my higher self with my lower self. It is a day for me to refine and fine tune my life by looking at my extremes. I recognize what inspires me and what keeps me stuck. I find my center today by acknowledging my extremes. I am aware that balance comes to those who are able to locate the space in the center of these opposite energy fields. When I am in my center, my polarities are in motion. Healing cannot occur unless my polarities are moving and I know that healing is motion.

I am ready for a healing today and know that by visiting my opposites and determining their vast opposition to each other, I can find the paradoxes that I have chosen for myself and begin to heal. I am willing to experiment with this blending of opposites and become the alchemist of my own life. When I blend all aspects of myself, rather than separating them, I can truly become whole. Today is a day to integrate, rather than separate, in order to release the spark of light that stays prisoner when my polarities are in operation. When I find balance, motion occurs and the Law of Harmony takes over, putting paradoxical energies to rest, thus breaking the crystallization of polarity. The Law of Harmony is beauty in motion, promoting the flow of color, light, sound, and movement into form. Balance is a condition that keeps my spark in motion. I become the vertical line in the center of polarity today and carry the secret of balance. Balance cannot be my goal, motion is my goal today. When I am in motion, I can take action to evolve and to express all of myself freely.

Sagittarius Homework

Now is the time to use your physical body to release the feeling of being caged in by people or circumstances. Choose an activity that burns away confinement and allows you to feel the power of your passion.

The Sagittarius moon awakens us to know the spark of light that lives in our heart, thus elevating love in ourselves and in our world. This is when we come to realize what is in our highest and best good and we can begin to recalibrate all that is not lovable in our lives.

Recalibrating List

Say this statement out loud three times before writing your recalibrating list:

I am a free spiritual being and it is my desire to be free to think and to express myself fully.

I am now free and ready to make choices beyond survival!

Sagittarius Recalibrating Ideas

Now is the time to activate a game change in my life, and give up belief systems that no longer apply, attitudes that are not uplifting to me, addiction to excess and risk, the need to exaggerate based on low self-esteem, dishonesty, being too blunt, staying in the future and avoiding the NOW, overriding fear by being too optimistic, and preaching.

Activate Acceleration

By acknowledging what you have recalibrated and overcome, you activate your acceleration. Keep this list active during this moon cycle.

Sky Power Yoga

Seated Pure Hip

You need one chair for the prop.

Sit one hand-width forward from the back of the chair. Back is straight and feet are placed hip-width apart on the floor. If your feet require more solid contact with the floor, place pillows or folded towels under your feet.

Bring your right foot up over your left knee. Rest your right ankle on your lower-left thigh.

Relax. Close your eyes. Breathe in and out slowly and deeply several times through your nose with your awareness on your thigh.

Inhale deeply and lengthen your back. Say or think to yourself the mantra *I Seek*.

Exhale slowly as you hinge at the hips and shift your weight gently forward.

Remain for several breaths. Inhale, engage your abdominals, and return your upper torso to an upright position. Repeat as desired.

Full Moon in Sagittarius

How to Use the Moon Book With Your Chart

Fill in the blanks on the Cosmic Check-In page. Then look up the degree of the Moon on the chart below. Take note of the "I" statement on the outside of the wheel where the Moon is located. Now, locate the same degree on your own chart and make a note of the house and corresponding

"I" statement. Go back to the Cosmic Check-In page and circle the two statements from the charts and read what you wrote. This will give you an idea about what to expect from this moon phase on a personal level.

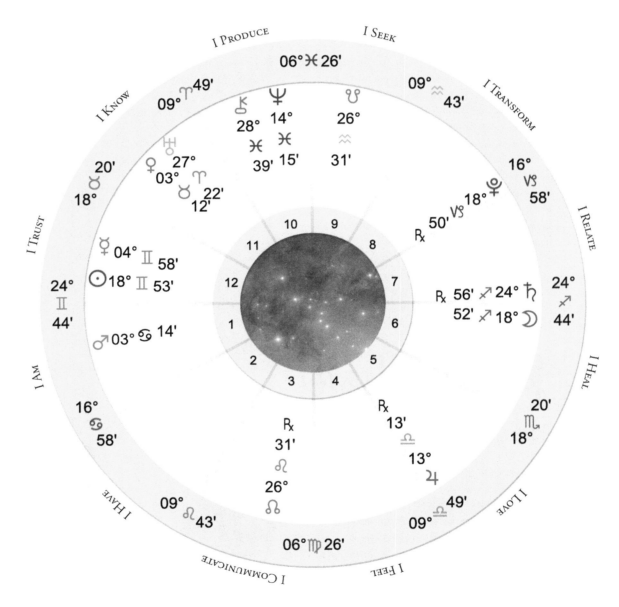

♈ Aries	♋ Cancer	♐ Sagittarius
♉ Taurus	♌ Leo	♑ Capricorn
♊ Gemini	♍ Virgo	♒ Aquarius
	♎ Libra	♓ Pisces
	♏ Scorpio	☉ Sun

☽ Moon	♄ Saturn	☊ North Node
☿ Mercury	♅ Uranus	☋ South Node
♀ Venus	♆ Neptune	➡ Enters
♂ Mars	♇ Pluto	℞ Retrograde
♃ Jupiter	⚷ Chiron	S/D Stationary Direct

V/C Void-of-Course
▲ Super-Sensitivity
▼ Low-Vitality

110

Cosmic Check-in

Take a moment to write a brief phrase for each "I" statement. This activates all areas of your life for this creative cycle.

⚹ I Seek

♑ I Produce

♒ I Know

♓ I Trust

♈ I Am

♉ I Have

♊ I Communicate

♋ I Feel

♌ I Love

♍ I Heal

♎ I Relate

♏ I Transform

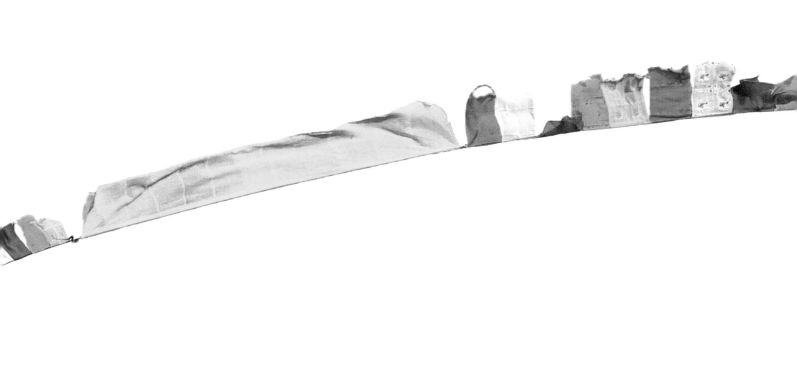

New Moon in Cancer

June 23rd, 7:30 PM

Statement I Feel

Body Stomach

Mind Worry

Spirit Nurturing

Element Water – Grace, rhythm, cycles of awareness, and the divine feminine.

Degree Choice Points
2° Cancer 46'

Light Mutual Success

Shadow Lack of Provisions

Wisdom Base your beliefs on your own experience and you will always have enough.

Seventh House Moon
26° Gemini 55'

Seventh House Umbrella Theme
I Feel/I Relate – One-on-one relationships, defines your people attraction force, and how you work in relationships with the people you attract.

Light Natural Rhythms

Shadow Halted Growth

Wisdom Base your beliefs on your own experience and you will always have enough.

Karmic Awakening

The Cancer/Capricorn polarity introduces the choice to be focused on personal or professional concerns.

When the Sun is in Cancer

It is now time to build our structure and foundation. Cancer holds the wisdom of the Great Cosmic Architect. Her statement is, "I build a lighted house and therein I dwell." The key is to use the materials of light, love, and wisdom to build your house and become the creator of form. Look within to see what lights your home and your body. Also check security systems, early environmental training, and mother/child relationships to see what materials you are using to build the structure for your life. Use this creating moon to build the structure you want.

Cancer Goddess

Hecate is a household goddess who assists people at times of transitions, such as childbirth and death. She is depicted as holding a torch to light the way when you reach major crossroads in life. Associated with the Underworld and the bridge into death and rebirth, Hecate is often shown with three heads and a loyal dog at her side. Her ability to see through the veil of illusion allowed her to assist Demeter in her search for Persephone, because Hecate could see into Hades. She rules over the earth, sea, and sky.

Are you, or someone in your household, feeling restless or aimless? Call upon Hecate's ability to clear the pathway through discernment, the wisdom that comes with age, and the knowledge of cycles.

Build Your Altar

Colors Shades of gray, milky/creamy colors

Numerology 7 – Love learning

Tarot Card Chariot – The ability to move forward, victory through action

Gemstones Pearl, moonstone, ruby

Plant Remedy Shooting Star – The ability to move straight ahead

Fragrance Peppermint – The essence of the Great Mother

Cancer Victories and Challenges

Say all of the statements in this section out loud. Then, underline the phrase that means the most to you. Use the phrase as your special affirmation for manifesting throughout this phase of the moon.

Today I take advantage of my ability to take action and position myself for success. I clearly know that the road to success is before me, and all I need to do is move forward. I am aware that when I take action and move forward, the Universe fills in the dots. Whether I move left, right, or straight ahead doesn't matter—what matters is movement. Today, I release the indecisiveness that keeps me stuck. Today, I let go of vacillation that exhausts my mind. Today, I take my foot off of the brakes and find the gas pedal. I allow movement to occur, even if I don't know where I am going. When I take action, I trust that guideposts will appear. I am aware that action leads me to my new direction. So, today I know and GO! I remember that Karma comes to the space of non-action, while success comes through action. Action brings me to my victory. Standing still leads to regret, resentment, and chaos.

I am aware that action can be as simple as taking a walk on the beach, buying fresh flowers to add a new dimension to my home, or simply going to a new restaurant for lunch. I take action today to break up a crystallized pattern and, in so doing, my life begins to show me newfound awareness and light to guide me.

Cancer Homework

Cancers manifest best when catering, writing cookbooks, in marriage and family counseling, providing childcare, giving massage, or when engaged in genealogy, arts and crafts, architecture, and home-building.

During the Cancer new moon cycle, we are asked to create light into form and turn it into beauty on four levels. Physically, we must feel nurtured and protected. Emotionally, we must set safe boundaries for the expression of our feelings. Mentally, we must release self-pity and embrace rightful thinking. Spiritually, we must hold the space for the infusion of light to shine inside all bodies on Earth.

Manifesting List

This or something better than this comes to me in an easy and pleasurable way, for the good of all concerned. Thank you, Universe!

Cancer Manifesting Ideas

Now is the time to focus on manifesting being a good mother, new ways to be a mom, nurturing and self-love, the ability to see joy, a clutter-free home, your dream home, and inner and outer security.

Gratitude List

Keep this list active throughout the moon cycle. This will bring you to a level of completion so that a new cycle of opportunity can occur in your life. Be prepared for miracles!

Sky Power Yoga

Child's Pose

You need two bath towels and one to two pillows for the prop.

Fold the two towels in half lengthwise, roll them into a log, and place them on the floor. Put both pillows on top of the rolled towels to support you in the pose.

Begin kneeling, placing your support prop in front of your knees then come onto hands and knees. Align your knees under your hips and your hands under your shoulders.

Close your eyes. Breathe in and out slowly and deeply several times through your nose with your awareness on your stomach.

Exhale and drop your hips back towards your heels so your front torso lowers onto the support prop. Slide your hands forward slightly and rest your head on the support prop. Turn your head to whichever side is most comfortable.

Inhale deeply. Exhale slowly as you say or think to yourself the mantra *I Feel*.

Relax fully into the support prop and the pose. Remain with the mantra and breath as long as desired.

New Moon in Cancer

How to Use the Moon Book With Your Chart

Fill in the blanks on the Cosmic Check-In page. Then look up the degree of the Moon on the chart below. Take note of the "I" statement on the outside of the wheel where the Moon is located. Now, locate the same degree on your own chart and make a note of the house and corresponding

"I" statement. Go back to the Cosmic Check-In page and circle the two statements from the charts and read what you wrote. This will give you an idea about what to expect from this moon phase on a personal level.

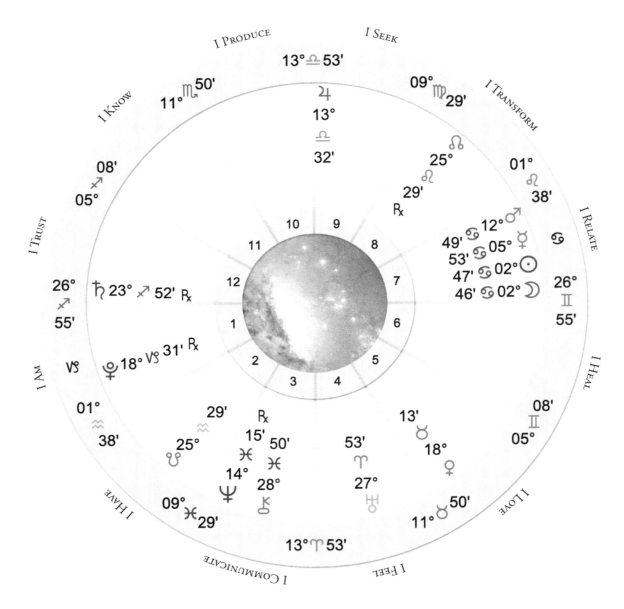

♈ Aries	♋ Cancer	♐ Sagittarius
♉ Taurus	♌ Leo	♑ Capricorn
♊ Gemini	♍ Virgo	♒ Aquarius
	♎ Libra	♓ Pisces
	♏ Scorpio	☉ Sun

☽ Moon	♄ Saturn	☊ North Node
☿ Mercury	♅ Uranus	☋ South Node
♀ Venus	♆ Neptune	➡ Enters
♂ Mars	♇ Pluto	℞ Retrograde
♃ Jupiter	⚷ Chiron	S/D Stationary Direct

V/C Void-of-Course	
▲ Super-Sensitivity	
▼ Low-Vitality	

Cosmic Check-in

Take a moment to write a brief phrase for each "I" statement. This activates all areas of your life for this creative cycle.

♋ I Feel

♌ I Love

♍ I Heal

♎ I Relate

♏ I Transform

♐ I Seek

♑ I Produce

♒ I Know

♓ I Trust

♈ I Am

♉ I Have

♊ I Communicate

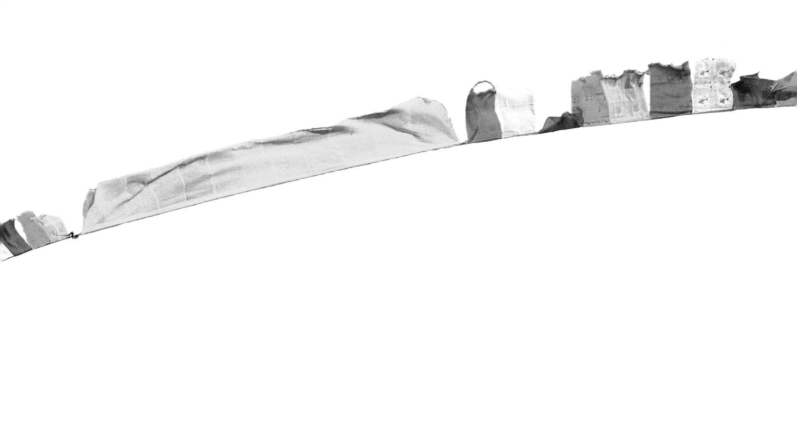

July

Planetary Highlights

Until August 25: Saturn retrograde in Sagittarius

Gain power from balancing the strength of the primal world by harmonizing it with the strength of your practical mind.

Until September 28: Pluto retrograde in Capricorn

Authority is transforming to create different systems. Move beyond your stubborn side to prevent the transformational energies accelerating beyond you. Accept the third stage of Capricorn's evolution to embrace the unicorn's power of magical intention.

Until November 22: Neptune retrograde in Pisces

Don't be lazy and believe others who say that they will take care of you. Live your truth to take care of yourself.

Until December 4: Chiron retrograde in Pisces

Heal yourself by healing your relationship with the spiritual world. Peace exists on earth when we release exclusionary religious practices. Take responsibility for your own spiritual growth and let religion keep rituals and ceremonies alive that peacefully bring people together.

July 4: Venus enters Gemini

Sharpen your flirting ability. Expect great conversations and have a blast at a party!

July 5: Mercury enters Leo

Write love letters and read love stories.

July 7-8: Super Sensitivity

Breathe. Mental overload could lead to disaster. Avoid thinking too much and take a yoga class instead.

July 8: Sun and Mars coupled in Cancer opposite Moon and Pluto in Capricorn

What stories do you tell about your relationship with your family? Expect a new storyline to break through that sets you free from old limitations and outdated plots.

July 20: Mars enters Leo

Expand your capacity for love and celebrate your creativity.

July 20-21: Low Vitality

Get rest or being habitually cranky could make you unpopular. Avoid stress. The issues at hand do not belong to you individually, but are global energy fields.

July 22: Sun enters Leo

Get out your dancing shoes as happy days are here again!

July 23: Venus opposite Saturn retrograde in Sagittarius

If you go shopping today, you'll just return everything tomorrow. Don't waste your time.

July 23: Mercury conjunct North Node in Leo

Pay attention as your mind sets up its future focus. What is on the horizon for you?

July 25: Mercury enters Virgo

Pay attention to the details and improve your life!

July 30-31: Low Vitality

Get rest or being habitually cranky could make you unpopular. Avoid stress. The issues at hand do not belong to you individually, but are global energy fields.

July 31: Venus enters Cancer

Enjoying time with family is your priority.

Sunday	Monday	Tuesday	Wednesday	Thursday	Friday	Saturday
						1 ♄♆⚷♇℞ 6. To have a friend, be a friend.
2 ♄♆⚷♇℞ ☽V/C 6:16 AM ☽→♏ 9:59 AM 7. Be flexible in your thinking.	**3** ♄♆⚷♇℞ 8. Success is meant to be celebrated.	**4** ♄♆⚷♇℞ Independence Day ☽V/C 6:34 PM ☽→♐ 10:07 PM ♀→♊ 5:13 PM 9. Connect with your heart in prayer.	**5** ♄♆⚷♇℞ ☿→♌ 5:21 PM 10. Live totally in the present.	**6** ♄♆⚷♇℞ 2. To be whole, connect all parts.	**7** ♄♆⚷♇℞ ▲ ☽V/C 7:11 AM ☽→♑ 10:44 AM 3. Things go better with laughter.	**8** ♄♆⚷♇℞ ▲ ○ 17°♑09' 9:06 PM 4. Sand is not a solid foundation.
9 ♄♆⚷♇℞ ☽V/C 7:12 PM ☽→♒ 10:34 PM 5. Give flexibility a chance.	**10** ♄♆⚷♇℞ 6. Choose food to nourish your body.	**11** ♄♆⚷♇℞ 7. Keep looking, you have the answer.	**12** ♄♆⚷♇℞ ☽V/C 5:40 AM ☽→♓ 8:51 AM 8. Intention supports success.	**13** ♄♆⚷♇℞ 9. Pray from your heart.	**14** ♄♆⚷♇℞ ☽V/C 10:00 AM ☽→♈ 4:52 PM 10. Drop the past.	**15** ♄♆⚷♇℞ 2. Use intuition to make a choice.
16 ♄♆⚷♇℞ ☽V/C 7:19 PM ☽→♉ 10:04 PM 3. Find joy in all that you do.	**17** ♄♆⚷♇℞ 4. Loyalty is the answer.	**18** ♄♆⚷♇℞ ☽V/C 11:11 PM 5. Do some car maintenance today.	**19** ♄♆⚷♇℞ ☽→♊ 12:31 AM 6. Share your space with friends.	**20** ♄♆⚷♇℞ ▼ ☽V/C 10:40 PM ♂→♌ 5:21 AM 7. Choose to learn something new.	**21** ♄♆⚷♇℞ ▼ ☽→♋ 1:09 AM 8. Trust in the law of circulation.	**22** ♄♆⚷♇℞ ☽V/C 11:04 PM ☉→♌ 8:16 AM 9. You are a spirit with a body.
23 ♄♆⚷♇℞ ● 0°♌44' 2:45AM ☽→♌ 1:33 AM 10. Stick to it, you will succeed.	**24** ♄♆⚷℞ 2. Remember to act on your intuition.	**25** ♄♆⚷♇℞ ☽V/C 2:21AM ☽→♍ 3:32 AM ☿→♍ 4:42 AM 3. Take the action that gives you joy.	**26** ♄♆⚷♇℞ ☽V/C 11:30 PM 4. Connecting details gives structure.	**27** ♄♆⚷♇℞ ☽→♎ 8:36 AM 5. Where can you find an adventure?	**28** ♄♆⚷♇℞ 6. Surprise a friend, take them to lunch.	**29** ♄♆⚷♇℞ ☽V/C 2:29 PM ☽→♏ 5:22 PM 7. When needed, ask for advice.
30 ♄♆⚷♇℞ ▼ 8. Just for fun, pay someone's way.	**31** ♄♆⚷♇℞ ▼ ☽V/C 4:10 AM ♀→♋ 7:55 AM 9. Donate to your favorite charity.					

♈ Aries	♎ Libra	☉ Sun	♄ Saturn	☊ North Node	▲ Super Sensitivity	6. Love
♉ Taurus	♏ Scorpio	☽ Moon	♅ Uranus	☋ South Node	▼ Low Vitality	7. Learning
♊ Gemini	♐ Sagittarius	☿ Mercury	♆ Neptune	➡ Enters	2. Balance	8. Money
♋ Cancer	♑ Capricorn	♀ Venus	♇ Pluto	℞ Retrograde	3. Fun	9. Spirituality
♌ Leo	♒ Aquarius	♂ Mars	⚷ Chiron	S/D Stationary Direct	4. Structure	10. Visionary
♍ Virgo	♓ Pisces	♃ Jupiter		V/C Void-of-Course	5. Action	11. Completion

Full Moon in Capricorn

July 8th, 9:06 PM

Statement I Produce
Body Knees
Mind Authority Issues
Spirit Self-reliance
Element Earth – Determination, endurance, stability, structured, over-pragmatic, practical, and stubborn.

Degree Choice Points
17° Capricorn 9'

Light Protection
Shadow Domination
Wisdom Become your own authority as looking outside yourself might not work.

Twelfth House Moon
10° Capricorn 10'

Twelfth House Umbrella Theme
I Trust/I Produce – Determines how you deal with your karma, unconscious software, and what you will experience in order to attain mastery by completing your karma. It is also about the way that you connect with the Divine.

Light Ambition
Shadow Mediocrity
Wisdom Read a book that is outside your usual reading habits.

The Sun is Opposite the Moon

Full moons are always in opposition to the Sun. This creates a feeling of tension between where you want to shine and how your feelings are flowing on a sensory level about the Sun's directive. The two forces seem like they are working against each other, yet they are on the same team displaying different techniques to obtain the same mission. The Capricorn/Cancer polarity creates tension between the quest for status and the need to feel secure.

Capricorn Goddess

The Goddess of hearth and home, Hestia, was once known as Chief of the Goddesses, and Hestia, the First and Last. Representing the central source, she embodies the virtues of a calm, stable, supportive, and well-centered mother and loving home-base. Hestia's symbols are the sacred flame and the circle. Choosing to stay home on Mount Olympus, she manages the estate and dependably provides a safe haven of unconditional love for all, even strangers. Connected by an umbilical cord at Delphi to the molten core of the Earth, Hestia's hearth flame will never be extinguished.

Allow your energy to tap into that root, running directly to the center of the Earth, and energize your ability to source and sustain your vision of your home, your community, and the Earth as sacred sanctuary.

Build Your Altar

Colors Forest green, earth tones
Numerology 4 – Sand is not a solid foundation
Tarot Card Devil – Confinement, attachment to form, look at the broader view
Gemstones Smoky quartz, topaz, garnet
Plant remedy Rosemary – Activates appropriate memory
Fragrance Frankincense – Assists the Soul's entry into the body

Clearing the Slate

Sixty hours before the full moon negative traits connected to the astro-sign might become activated to trigger what needs to be released during the full moon phase. You may notice a sudden burden of responsibility taking over your experience of life, of paying too much attention to status and position, of no time to feel compassionate, and of challenging authorities. Make a list of the triggers and do Ho'oponopono, a Hawaiian Huna ritual for forgiveness. Look in the mirror, and for each negative trait, tell yourself *I am sorry, I forgive you, thank you for your awareness,* and *I love you.*

Capricorn Victories and Challenges

Say all of the statements in this section out loud. Then, underline the phrase that means the most to you. Use the phrase as your special affirmation for recalibrating throughout this phase of the moon.

I feel limited. I feel confined. I feel stuck. I feel there is no way out. Perhaps I am the target of someone's envy or jealousy, or perhaps I am jealous or I am envious. Maybe I am spending too much time in the outer world and putting too much value on material rewards, things, and possessions. Maybe I am trying to possess someone or limit their view or choice. I may feel there are no choices. Maybe I am living by someone else's rules and beliefs and forgot how to think for myself. I could also be overcome by fear and too terrorized to look at anything at all.

Today, I see and feel the limits of placing the source of love outside myself. I have tunnel vision and I seem to have forgotten to look at my options. I must ask myself today, "How many ways can I look at my life, my situation, or my perceived problems?" Today, I must expand my view to encompass 360-degrees instead of only 180-degrees. I begin by acknowledging to myself that today is the worst it is going to get. I know deep within me that if I allow myself to truly experience my bottom, the top will become visible to me. It is time to look at the brighter side. Begin by identifying the problem by writing it down on a piece of paper. Start with the phrase, "The problem is_____." Fill in the blank. Then, list as many solutions to the problem as you can. List at least three. Then, say these solutions out loud every day until the answer comes to you through a person, an idea, an event, or a choice.

Capricorn Homework

Put on a good pair of walking shoes and get ready to walk your blues away. It is time to get outside and feel the loving power of Mother Earth. The green of the trees refreshes your stagnant energy while you exhaust yourself to a point of vulnerability. Then, and only then, will you feel freedom. Give yourself permission to throw your watch away and learn to live in the moment.

The Capricorn moon is the reincarnation of Spirit emerging from the dark waters of our past emotions and releasing us from our fear of change and our fear of loss. Awaken your powerful and positive spiritual connection to be open to new possibilities. Ask yourself to release your emotional loyalty to the past. We are reminded of our need for material and emotional security at this time. In order to ensure this, we must learn to build a foundation for ourselves that is lit from within, made from the materials of love, goodwill, and intelligence.

Recalibrating List

Say this statement out loud three times before writing your recalibrating list:

I am a free spiritual being and it is my desire to be free to think and to express myself fully.

From this day forward I resolve to be true – first to myself and my highest self,
and then to the highest self in me which is the Source of Love That I Am.

Capricorn Recalibrating Ideas

Now is the time to activate a game change in my life, and give up obstacles to success, authority issues, sorrow and sadness, fear that blocks me, arrogance, irritability, limitations of time, priorities that are no longer valid, control and domination, the need to do it all alone, and taking on excessive responsibility.

Activate Acceleration

By acknowledging what you have recalibrated and overcome, you activate your acceleration. Keep this list active during this moon cycle.

Sky Power Yoga

Seated Egg Beaters

You need two bath towels and one or more pillows for the prop.

Nest two towels, fold in quarters, and place on the chair. Place the pillow on top of the towels. Sit on the chair to see if your feet hang freely without touching the floor. Add additional pillows or folded towels to elevate you so that your feet don't touch the floor.

Sit one hand-width forward from the back of the chair. Back is straight and head is neutral. Reach behind with both hands to hold the side edges of the chair.

Relax. Close your eyes. Breathe in and out slowly several times through your nose with your awareness on your knees.

Swing your feet forward, out, and around with each foot circling in the opposite direction like an egg beater. The right foot circles clockwise, the left counterclockwise. Allow the movement of the right foot to propel the left. This movement gives a relaxing

massage to the knee joint and surrounding muscles.

Inhale deeply and say or think the mantra *I Produce.*

Exhale as you slowly circle your feet. Once your breath is fully exhaled, pause, and repeat as desired.

Full Moon in Capricorn

How to Use the Moon Book With Your Chart

Fill in the blanks on the Cosmic Check-In page. Then look up the degree of the Moon on the chart below. Take note of the "I" statement on the outside of the wheel where the Moon is located. Now, locate the same degree on your own chart and make a note of the house and corresponding

"I" statement. Go back to the Cosmic Check-In page and circle the two statements from the charts and read what you wrote. This will give you an idea about what to expect from this moon phase on a personal level.

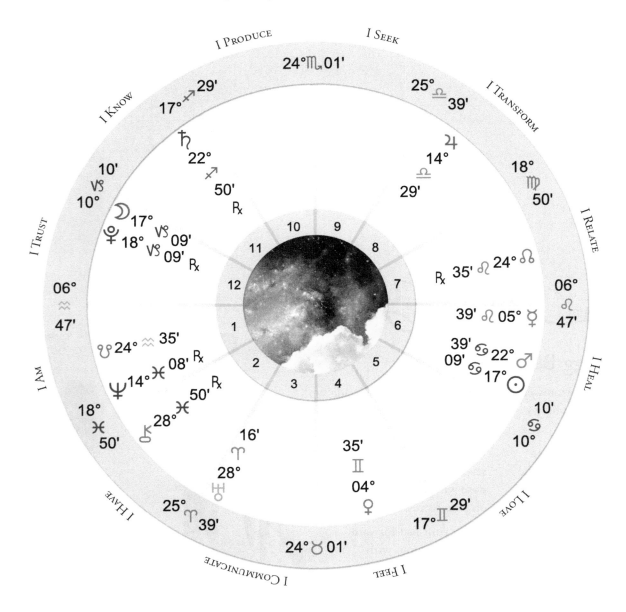

♈	Aries	♋	Cancer	♐	Sagittarius
♉	Taurus	♌	Leo	♑	Capricorn
♊	Gemini	♍	Virgo	♒	Aquarius
		♎	Libra	♓	Pisces
		♏	Scorpio		

☽	Moon	♄	Saturn	☊	North Node
☿	Mercury	♅	Uranus	☋	South Node
♀	Venus	♆	Neptune	➡	Enters
♂	Mars	♇	Pluto	℞	Retrograde
☉	Sun	⚷	Chiron	S/D	Stationary Direct
♃	Jupiter				

V/C	Void-of-Course
▲	Super-Sensitivity
▼	Low-Vitality

Cosmic Check-in

Take a moment to write a brief phrase for each "I" statement. This activates all areas of your life for this creative cycle.

♑ I Produce

♒ I Know

♓ I Trust

♈ I Am

♉ I Have

♊ I Communicate

♋ I Feel

♌ I Love

♍ I Heal

♎ I Relate

♏ I Transform

♐ I Seek

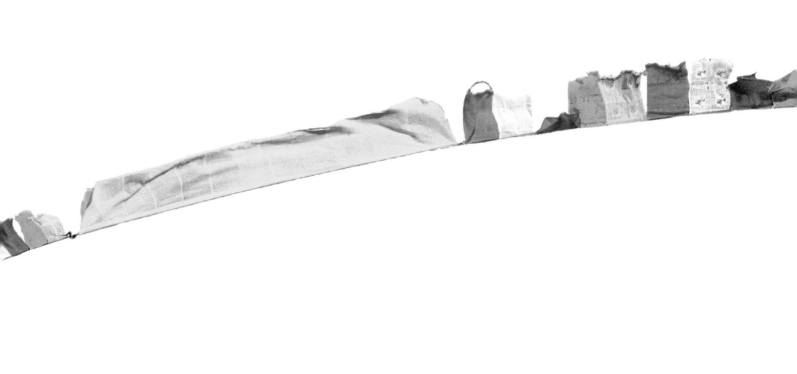

New Moon in Leo

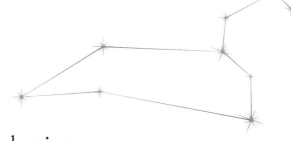

July 23rd, 2:45 AM

Statement I Love

Body Heart

Mind Self-confidence

Spirit Generosity

Element Fire – Passion, enthusiasm, warmth, and personal identity-centered.

Degree Choice Points

0° Leo 43'

Light Creative Self-expression

Shadow Imposing Will

Wisdom Add a piece to the puzzle to find the new configuration.

Second House Moon

10° Cancer 6'

Second House Umbrella Theme

I Have/I Feel – The way you make your money and the way you spend it.

Light Humorous

Shadow Camouflage

Wisdom Hold the light for another to help them find their way.

Karmic Awakening

Karma gets activated when personal and professional focus is confused. Review your motivation to determine correct action.

When the Sun is in Leo

This is the time when you feel the power from the Sun, the heart of the Cosmos. Leo has a direct relationship with the Sun's heart. The Sun rules your identity. Now is the time to shine and stand tall in the center of your life. Allow yourself to feel the power of your individual conscious Self. When you align with the power of the Sun, you become radiant. This radiance gives you the power to transmit energy into life. Personal fulfillment becomes a reality when you align your will with love. Remember to live love every day!

Leo Goddess

Aphrodite sashays into the Summer party, full of moxie and ready to flirt! The Goddess of Beauty and Love is enlivening all aspects of your life with joyful play!

Get into your Feminine Light. Giggle, dance, and sing! What a great time for a girl's night out or karaoke on the beach beside a roaring bonfire! Work it! Swish your skirts and strut your stuff! Tap into Aphrodite's inner light for fun and frolic. Aphrodite reminds us that play is also our spiritual work. Bring some joy and fun into it!

Build Your Altar

Colors Royal purple, royal blue, orange

Numerology 10 – Let acceleration take you to your next step

Tarot Card Sun – To stand tall in the center of life

Gemstones Peridot, emerald, amber

Plant Remedy Sunflower – Standing tall in the center of your garden

Fragrance Jasmine – Remembering your Soul's original intention

Leo Victories and Challenges

Say all of the statements in this section out loud. Then, underline the phrase that means the most to you. Use the phrase as your special affirmation for manifesting throughout this phase of the moon.

Today, I am at the center of bliss, happiness, abundance, and total celebration. It is my time to shine and feel the power of my true self blasting the Universe, the entire planet, and all of life with the light of my awareness. There is nothing that can stop me today, because I am free to be me. When I am free to be me, I can stand naked in the daylight and have nothing to hide. I truly know that all of life loves me and I love all of life. I feel the radiance and vibration of my being activating me with aliveness, vitality, and charisma. I know that I can make a difference because I celebrate life by infusing, sparking, and igniting matter with light. I am open and ready to embrace all that comes to me with joy. I say "YES!" to all opportunities today; knowing that today is my day. I am in the flow of abundance and I let abundance flow through me.

The child within me is open and ready to play full out; there is not a cloud in the sky today that can eclipse me or place a shadow on me and keep me from my true level of power. I am aware that the child state of being within me simply says yes to action and action is power. When I take action today, my possibilities are endless because they are generated from my true self and motivated by happiness, joy, and freedom. The child within me is able to play full out because I have birthed myself beyond my old perception of blocks. I know that in taking this true power, to be motivated by happiness, pathways on all levels and in all dimensions can open to the empowerment of joy. Empowerment is mine today because I am shining from within myself and I know my deepest self is connected to the source. Empowerment occurs when I live from the inside out. Today, I wave the banner of my being from within, feel the glow, and go.

Leo Homework

Leos manifest best through fashion and jewelry design, glamour, politics, super-modeling, movie stardom, child advocacy, fundraising, toy and game design, image consulting, authoring children's books, sales, and cardiology.

Leo gets you closer to your essential self, reminding you of your Soul's original intention. You become ready to receive the benefits of reflective light and radiating light at the same time, so that you can see your personality and your Soul connecting to love which constitutes a new level of fulfillment. Expect purification, transmutation, communication, and mastery to be part of your personal experience.

Manifesting List

This or something better than this comes to me in an easy and pleasurable way, for the good of all concerned. Thank you, Universe!

Leo Manifesting Ideas

Now is the time to focus on manifesting new love or new ways of loving, new creative ways of expressing myself, bonding with those I love, quality time with those I love, knowledge of my Soul's intention, fun with my children, being a bright beaming light, and connecting to the hearts of humanity.

Gratitude List

Keep this list active throughout the moon cycle. This will bring you to a level of completion so that a new cycle of opportunity can occur in your life. Be prepared for miracles!

Sky Power Yoga

Seated Cactus Arms

You need one chair for the prop.

Sit one hand-width forward from the chair back with your feet on the floor hip-width apart. Feet should have solid contact with the floor. Use pillows or folded towels to support your feet, if necessary.

Lengthen your spine to straighten your back. To make the cactus arms, lift and bend arms so that your hands are at a 90 degree angle from your elbow.

Relax and close your eyes. Breathe in and out slowly and deeply several times through your nose maintaining your awareness on your heart center.

Inhale deeply and squeeze your shoulder blades together, then press elbows back, and lift your sternum slightly. Say or think to yourself the mantra *I Love.*

Exhale slowly. Bring your elbows together and round your back slightly. Your body does a subtle back bend as you inhale and a subtle forward bend as you exhale. Repeat as desired.

New Moon in Leo

How to Use the Moon Book With Your Chart

Fill in the blanks on the Cosmic Check-In page. Then look up the degree of the Moon on the chart below. Take note of the "I" statement on the outside of the wheel where the Moon is located. Now, locate the same degree on your own chart and make a note of the house and corresponding

"I" statement. Go back to the Cosmic Check-In page and circle the two statements from the charts and read what you wrote. This will give you an idea about what to expect from this moon phase on a personal level.

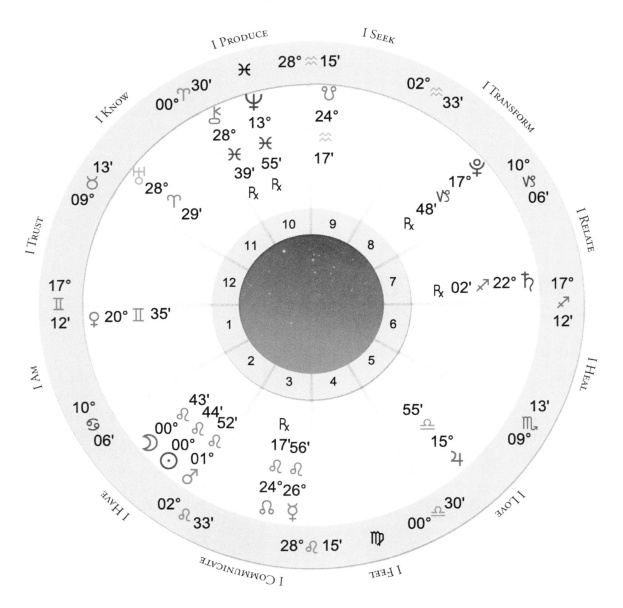

♈	Aries	♋	Cancer	♐	Sagittarius	☽	Moon	♄	Saturn	☊	North Node	V/C Void-of-Course
♉	Taurus	♌	Leo	♑	Capricorn	☿	Mercury	♅	Uranus	☋	South Node	▲ Super-Sensitivity
♊	Gemini	♍	Virgo	♒	Aquarius	♀	Venus	♆	Neptune	➡	Enters	▼ Low-Vitality
		♎	Libra	♓	Pisces	♂	Mars	♇	Pluto	℞	Retrograde	
		♏	Scorpio			☉	Sun	⚷	Chiron	S/D	Stationary Direct	

Cosmic Check-in

Take a moment to write a brief phrase for each "I" statement. This activates all areas of your life for this creative cycle.

♌ I Love

♍ I Heal

♎ I Relate

♏ I Transform

♐ I Seek

♑ I Produce

♒ I Know

♓ I Trust

♈ I Am

♉ I Have

♊ I Communicate

♋ I Feel

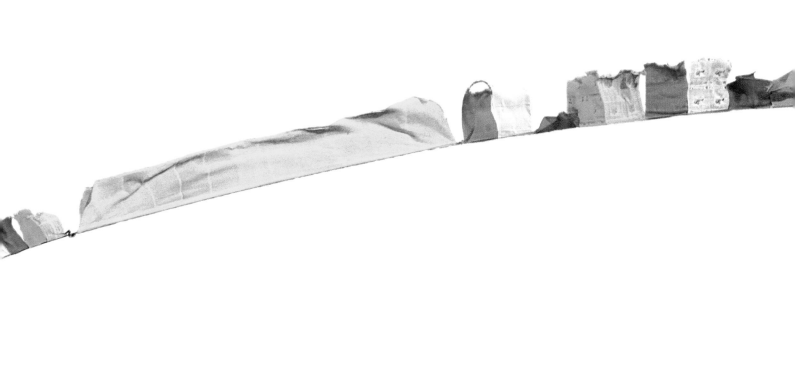

August

Planetary Highlights

Until August 25: Saturn retrograde in Sagittarius

The subtleties in life are as important as the large scale events.

Until September 28: Pluto retrograde in Capricorn

Get a financial planner to deal with any outstanding money issues. Stick to the plan to best take care of yourself.

Until November 22: Neptune retrograde in Pisces

Are you wearing rose-colored glasses? Face reality and recalibrate what's not working.

Until December 4: Chiron retrograde in Pisces

Which traditions or religions work for you? Which ones have lost their glow? Sort, sift, and release what doesn't spark you anymore. New inspiration arrives when you complete your review.

August 2: Uranus retrograde in Aries

This is a game changer well into 2018, as everything suddenly stops and does a sharp U-turn. The resulting shock waves show you your new direction and focus.

August 3-4: Super Sensitivity

Keep your boundaries straight and all will be well.

August 7-8: Sun and Mars coupled in Leo

Bright lights shine on all your actions. Use this high visibility to your advantage.

August 7-30: Mercury in Virgo opposite Neptune in Pisces

A period of important scientific discovery benefiting many people may occur.

August 12-September 5: Mercury retrograde in Virgo

Mercury retrograde is happy in Virgo. Tend to the details and your projects get good results or take on a research project that you enjoy.

August 17-18: Low Vitality

Get rest. Don't fight the need for calm.

August 21: North Node in Leo conjunct Mars

All will be good if you live love in each moment.

August 21: Jupiter in Libra opposite Uranus in Aries

From today and into 2018, know your boundaries so you don't get stuck.

August 22: Sun enters Virgo

Let the light of summer heal your body. Expect new healers and ways to take care of your health to bloom in your life.

August 25: Venus enters Leo

Keep dancing, live love, and let the summer fun continue!

August 31: Mercury enters Leo

Your mind and your heart blend in a deep expression of love. Let your heart speak for them both.

August 30-31: Super Sensitivity

Keep your boundaries straight and all will be well.

Sunday	Monday	Tuesday	Wednesday	Thursday	Friday	Saturday
		1 ♄♆⚷♇℞ ☽→♐ 5:01AM 10. Fully live in the now.	**2** ♄♆⚷♅♇℞ ♅S/R–28°♈31′ 10:32PM 2. Balance all aspects of your life.	**3** ♄♆⚷♅♇℞ ▲ ☽V/C 2:38 PM ☽→♑ 5:36 PM 3. Life is a cosmic joke, keep laughing.	**4** ♄♆⚷♅♇℞ ▲ 4. Make more progress by organizing.	**5** ♄♆⚷♅♇℞ 5. Make changes only as needed.
6 ♄♆⚷♅♇℞ ☽V/C 2:21 AM ☽→♒ 5:15 AM 6. Welcome your guests with joy.	**7** ♄♆⚷♅♇℞ ○ 15°♒25′ 11:10 AM Lunar Eclipse 11:24AM 7. Go with what works.	**8** ♄♆⚷♅♇℞ ☽V/C 12:07 PM ☽→♓ 2:55 PM 9. Pray for a posivite outcome.	**9** ♄♆⚷♅♇℞ 10. Your direction comes from within.	**10** ♄♆⚷♅♇℞ ☽V/C 6:37 AM ☽→♈ 10:21 PM 2. Forage forward, take action.	**11** ♄♆⚷♅♇℞ 3. Recycling serves a creative purpose.	**12** ☿♆⚷♄♅♇℞ ☿S/R–11°♍37″ 6:02PM 4. See the support in your surroundings.
13 ☿♆⚷♄♅♇℞ ☽V/C 1:00 AM ☽→♉ 3:39 AM 5. Make changes to eliminate toxins.	**14** ☿♆⚷♄♅♇℞ ☽V/C 6:15 PM 6. Listen to your body for answers.	**15** ☿♆⚷♄♅♇℞ ☽→♊ 7:06 AM 7. You are never too old to learn.	**16** ☿♆⚷♄♅♇℞ 8. Praise someone on their success.	**17** ☿♆⚷♄♅♇℞ ▼ ☽V/C 6:38 AM ☽→♋ 9:12 AM 9. Fulfill your mission with passion.	**18** ☿♆♄⚷♅♇℞ ▼ 10. All endings are new beginnings.	**19** ☿♆♄⚷♅♇℞ ☽V/C 8:16 AM ☽→♌ 10:54 AM 2. Slow down and find your balance.
20 ☿♆♄⚷♅♇℞ 3. Life is filled with creative purpose.	**21** ☿♆♄⚷♅♇℞ ● 28°♌53′ 11:30AM Solar Eclipse 11:28AM ☽V/C 11:30 AM ☽→♍ 1:24 PM 4. If it's logical, it's probably right.	**22** ☿♆♄⚷♅♇℞ ☉→♍ 3:21 PM 5. Ignite expansion in your life today.	**23** ☿♆♄⚷♅♇℞ ☽V/C 1:02 PM ☽→♎ 6:04 PM 6. Make your health a top priority.	**24** ☿♆♄⚷♅♇℞ 7. Learn something from someone else.	**25** ☿♆⚷♅♇℞ ☽V/C 10:39 PM ♄S/D–21°♐10′ 5:10AM ♀→♌ 9:31PM 8. Abundance is more than money.	**26** ☿♆⚷♅♇℞ ☽→♏ 1:52 AM 9. When you are inspired, act.
27 ☿♆♅⚷♇℞ 10. In order to move on, drop the past.	**28** ☿♆♅⚷♇℞ ☽V/C 2:37 AM ☽→♐ 12:47PM 2. One decision leads to another.	**29** ☿♆♅⚷♇℞ 3. There are many ways to be creative.	**30** ☿♆♅⚷♇℞ ▲ ☽V/C 9:42 PM 4. Be an active team player.	**31** ☿♆♅⚷♇℞ ▲ ☽→♑ 1:18 AM ♀→♌ 8:29AM 5. Take a different route, just for fun.		

♈ Aries	♎ Libra	☉ Sun	♄ Saturn	☊ North Node	▲ Super Sensitivity	6. Love
♉ Taurus	♏ Scorpio	☽ Moon	♅ Uranus	☋ South Node	▼ Low Vitality	7. Learning
♊ Gemini	♐ Sagittarius	☿ Mercury	♆ Neptune	➡ Enters	2. Balance	8. Money
♋ Cancer	♑ Capricorn	♀ Venus	♇ Pluto	℞ Retrograde	3. Fun	9. Spirituality
♌ Leo	♒ Aquarius	♂ Mars	⚷ Chiron	S/D Stationary Direct	4. Structure	10. Visionary
♍ Virgo	♓ Pisces	♃ Jupiter		V/C Void-of-Course	5. Action	11. Completion

Full Moon in Aquarius

August 7th, 11:10 AM
Lunar Eclipse

Statement I Know
Body Ankles
Mind True Genius
Spirit Vision
Element Air – Curiosity, learning, flexibility, and consciousness directed towards form.

Degree Choice Points
15° Aquarius 24'
Light Achievement
Shadow Superficial Achievement
Wisdom A supervised cleanse will release residues.

Fourth House Moon
22° Capricorn 44'
Fourth House Umbrella Theme
I Feel/I Produce – How your early environmental training was, how that set your foundation for living, and why you chose your mother.

Light Teamwork
Shadow Undermining
Wisdom Accept your uniqueness within the group.

The Sun is Opposite the Moon

Full moons are always in opposition to the Sun. This creates a feeling of tension between where you want to shine and how your feelings are flowing on a sensory level about the Sun's directive. The two forces seem like they are working against each other, yet they are on the same team displaying different techniques to obtain the same mission. The Aquarian/Leo polarity creates tension between the quest for group interaction and the recognition of self.

Aquarius Goddess

The Egyptian Goddess Maat ushers in a time of discovery about who you are at the core, as your most balanced and beneficent self, and about the work you came here to do in this lifetime. According to the Egyptian Book of the Dead, Maat is the goddess you visit upon your death. She places her single ostrich feather on the scale to be weighed against your heart. If you have lived a virtuous life, and reached your highest potential as a kind and decent human being, your heart will be as light as Maat's feather, and you would cross over. If not, you will be devoured by the Goddess Ammit and would be reborn into duality for another lifetime.

Let this moon show you your potential and re-orient yourself to your life's highest work and purpose. The Egyptian word for heart was "ib." Ask yourself, who will "I be" in this lifetime?

Build Your Altar

Colors Electric colors, neon, multi-colors, pearl white
Numerology 7 – Go with what works
Tarot Card Star – Being guided by a higher source
Gemstones Aquamarine, amethyst, opal
Plant remedy Queen of the Night Cactus – The ability to see in the dark
Fragrance Myrrh – Healing the nervous system

Clearing the Slate

Sixty hours before the full moon negative traits connected to the astro-sign might become activated to trigger what needs to be released during the full moon phase. You may notice yourself becoming stubborn, escaping reality by living in the future, and the need to be rebellious if you feel frenzied or chaotic. Make a list of the triggers and do Ho'oponopono, a Hawaiian Huna ritual for forgiveness. Look in the mirror, and for each negative trait, tell yourself *I am sorry, I forgive you, thank you for your awareness,* and *I love you.*

Aquarius Victories and Challenges

Say all of the statements in this section out loud. Then, underline the phrase that means the most to you. Use the phrase as your special affirmation for recalibrating throughout this phase of the moon.

Today my true potential can be realized. All I have to do is take a risk and know that my faith is in operation. My future is very bright and offers me a promise of things to come. Today is a day of destiny. I have chosen this day to determine a DESTINY PROMISE I MADE TO MYSELF BEFORE I CAME INTO THIS LIFE. All that is required of me is to move out of my comfort zone and take a risk. I am aware that faith cannot be determined without risk. I take the risk to move into the next space of creation in my life. I release fear and move into faith, knowing full well that my logic and reason are part of the fear that keeps me stuck.

I am reminded that the kingdom of heaven is open to the child. I find the child within me today to embrace what life has for me with open arms and a spirit of adventure. I know my true potential lives inside my magical child and she/he is willing to play and go for the gusto. I am here in this life to fulfill my promise to experience life to the fullest and to release the fear of judgment that has hounded me and kept me from playing full-out. I remember that when I experience, I gather a knowledge base within my Soul and keep my agreement with myself and the Universe. I connect to my super-consciousness and take on the bigger view of my life and all that it has to offer me when I risk reason and take a leap of faith. I know in the depth of my awareness that, if I jump off the diving board, there will be water in the pool. I am willing to risk reason for an experience. Everything I ever wanted is one step outside my comfort zone. I go for the GUSTO today! I release my fear today and turn it into faith. I trust in the promise of things to come. I know my potential is realized today, and that all I have to do is say "YES!" to life!

Aquarius Homework

The Aquarius moon reminds us of our connection to solar fire (the heart of the Sun) also known as the Heart of the Cosmos. During this time, we get our vitality recharged and our potent power comes into play motivating the masses to receive more energy to transmute into the new world. Voice all that you know to be true to the point of self-realization where your authentic purpose can be revealed to you. This is the moment where you have released all that has kept you from your true sense of freedom. Remember to replenish all the electrolytes in your system.

Recalibrating List

Say this statement out loud three times before writing your recalibrating list:

I am a free spiritual being and it is my desire to be free to think and to express myself fully.

Freedom is mine when I live my truth!

Aquarius Recalibrating Ideas

Now is the time to activate a game change in my life, and give up resistance to authority figures, blocks to living in the moment, unnecessary rebellion, non-productive frenzy and fantasy, the need to be spontaneous, and people who aren't team players.

Activate Acceleration

By acknowledging what you have recalibrated and overcome, you activate your acceleration. Keep this list active during this moon cycle.

Sky Power Yoga

Seated Ankle Rotations

You need one chair for the prop.

Sit in a chair with your back straight and your feet on the floor, hip-width apart. Feet should have solid contact with the floor. Use pillows or folded towels to support your feet, if necessary.

Rest your right ankle on your lower left thigh. Lace the fingers of your left hand between your right foot's toes. Your pinky finger goes between your outer two toes and so forth until your index finger is next to your big toe.

Relax. Close your eyes. Breathe in and out slowly and deeply several times through your nose with your awareness on the ankle.

Inhale deeply. Say or think the mantra *I Know.*

Exhale slowly while using your hand to guide the ball

of your foot in a circular motion, counterclockwise. Repeat as many times as feels comfortable and then switch to the other foot.

Full Moon in Aquarius

How to Use the Moon Book With Your Chart

Fill in the blanks on the Cosmic Check-In page. Then look up the degree of the Moon on the chart below. Take note of the "I" statement on the outside of the wheel where the Moon is located. Now, locate the same degree on your own chart and make a note of the house and corresponding

"I" statement. Go back to the Cosmic Check-In page and circle the two statements from the charts and read what you wrote. This will give you an idea about what to expect from this moon phase on a personal level.

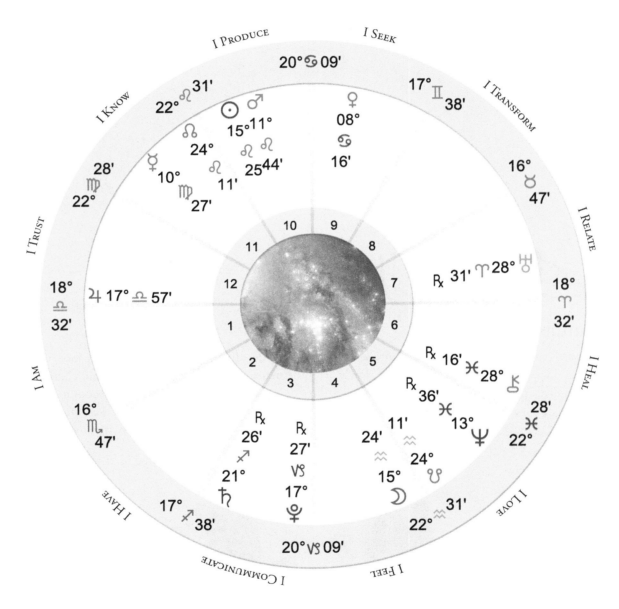

♈	Aries	♋	Cancer	♐	Sagittarius	☽	Moon	♄	Saturn	☊	North Node	V/C	Void-of-Course
♉	Taurus	♌	Leo	♑	Capricorn	☿	Mercury	♅	Uranus	☋	South Node	▲	Super-Sensitivity
♊	Gemini	♍	Virgo	♒	Aquarius	♀	Venus	♆	Neptune	➡	Enters	▼	Low-Vitality
		♎	Libra	♓	Pisces	♂	Mars	♇	Pluto	℞	Retrograde		
		♏	Scorpio	☉	Sun	♃	Jupiter	⚷	Chiron	S/D	Stationary Direct		

Cosmic Check-in

Take a moment to write a brief phrase for each "I" statement. This activates all areas of your life for this creative cycle.

♒ I Know

♓ I Trust

♈ I Am

♉ I Have

♊ I Communicate

♋ I Feel

♌ I Love

♍ I Heal

♎ I Relate

♏ I Transform

♐ I Seek

♑ I Produce

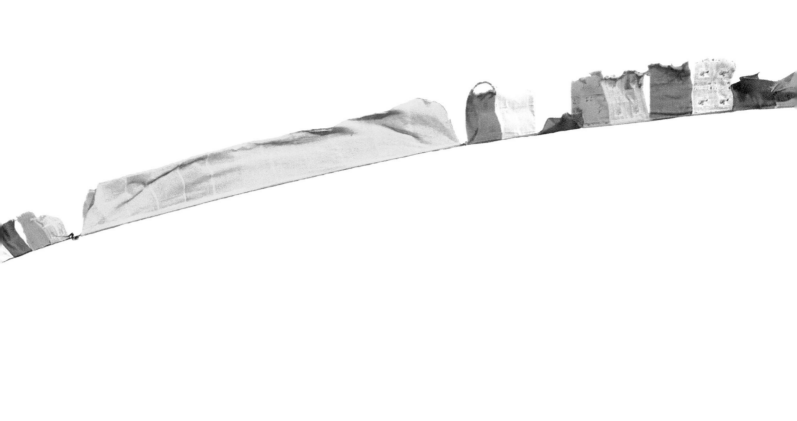

New Moon in Leo

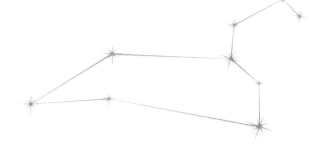

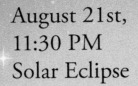

August 21st, 11:30 PM Solar Eclipse

Statement I Love
Body Heart
Mind Self-confidence
Spirit Generosity
Element Fire – Passion, enthusiasm, warmth, and personal identity-centered.

Degree Choice Points
28° Leo 53'
Light Finding Purpose
Shadow External Validation
Wisdom Recognize your life's purpose.

Tenth House Moon
8° Capricorn 11'
Tenth House Umbrella Theme
I Produce/I Love – Your approach to status, career, honor, and prestige, and why you chose your father.
Light Enthusiasm
Shadow Spinning the Truth
Wisdom Inspire progress.

When the Sun is in Leo

This is the time when you feel the power from the Sun, the heart of the Cosmos. Leo has a direct relationship with the Sun's heart. The Sun rules your identity. Now is the time to shine and stand tall in the center of your life. Allow yourself to feel the power of your individual conscious Self. When you align with the power of the Sun, you become radiant. This radiance gives you the power to transmit energy into life. Personal fulfillment becomes a reality when you align your will with love. Remember to live love every day!

Leo Goddess

Aphrodite sashays into the Summer party, full of moxie and ready to flirt! The Goddess of Beauty and Love is enlivening all aspects of your life with joyful play!

Get into your Feminine Light. Giggle, dance, and sing! What a great time for a girl's night out or karaoke on the beach beside a roaring bonfire! Work it! Swish your skirts and strut your stuff! Tap into Aphrodite's inner light for fun and frolic. Aphrodite reminds us that play is also our spiritual work. Bring some joy and fun into it!

Build Your Altar

Colors Royal purple, royal blue, orange
Numerology 4 – If it's logical, it's probably right
Tarot Card Sun – To stand tall in the center of life
Gemstones Peridot, emerald, amber
Plant Remedy Sunflower – Standing tall in the center of your garden
Fragrance Jasmine – Remembering your Soul's original intention

Leo Victories and Challenges

Say all of the statements in this section out loud. Then, underline the phrase that means the most to you. Use the phrase as your special affirmation for manifesting throughout this phase of the moon.

Today, I am at the center of bliss, happiness, abundance, and total celebration. It is my time to shine and feel the power of my true self blasting the Universe, the entire planet, and all of life with the light of my awareness. There is nothing that can stop me today, because I am free to be me. When I am free to be me, I can stand naked in the daylight and have nothing to hide. I truly know that all of life loves me and I love all of life. I feel the radiance and vibration of my being activating me with aliveness, vitality, and charisma. I know that I can make a difference because I celebrate life by infusing, sparking, and igniting matter with light. I am open and ready to embrace all that comes to me with joy. I say "YES!" to all opportunities today; knowing that today is my day. I am in the flow of abundance and I let abundance flow through me.

The child within me is open and ready to play full out; there is not a cloud in the sky today that can eclipse me or place a shadow on me and keep me from my true level of power. I am aware that the child state of being within me simply says yes to action and action is power. When I take action today, my possibilities are endless because they are generated from my true self and motivated by happiness, joy, and freedom. The child within me is able to play full out because I have birthed myself beyond my old perception of blocks. I know that in taking this true power, to be motivated by happiness, pathways on all levels and in all dimensions can open to the empowerment of joy. Empowerment is mine today because I am shining from within myself and I know my deepest self is connected to the source. Empowerment occurs when I live from the inside out. Today, I wave the banner of my being from within, feel the glow, and go.

Leo Homework

Leos manifest best through fashion and jewelry design, glamour, politics, super-modeling, movie stardom, child advocacy, fundraising, toy and game design, image consulting, authoring children's books, sales, and cardiology.

Leo gets you closer to your essential self, reminding you of your Soul's original intention. You become ready to receive the benefits of reflective light and radiating light at the same time, so that you can see your personality and your Soul connecting to love which constitutes a new level of fulfillment. Expect purification, transmutation, communication, and mastery to be part of your personal experience.

Manifesting List

This or something better than this comes to me in an easy and pleasurable way, for the good of all concerned. Thank you, Universe!

Leo Manifesting Ideas

Now is the time to focus on manifesting new love or new ways of loving, new creative ways of expressing myself, bonding with those I love, quality time with those I love, knowledge of my Soul's intention, fun with my children, being a bright beaming light, and connecting to the hearts of humanity.

Gratitude List

Keep this list active throughout the moon cycle. This will bring you to a level of completion so that a new cycle of opportunity can occur in your life. Be prepared for miracles!

Sky Power Yoga

Seated Cactus Arms

You need one chair for the prop.

Sit one hand-width forward from the chair back with your feet on the floor hip-width apart. Feet should have solid contact with the floor. Use pillows or folded towels to support your feet, if necessary.

Lengthen your spine to straighten your back. To make the cactus arms, lift and bend arms so that your hands are at a 90 degree angle from your elbow.

Relax and close your eyes. Breathe in and out slowly and deeply several

times through your nose maintaining your awareness on your heart center.

Inhale deeply and squeeze your shoulder blades together, then press elbows back, and lift your sternum slightly. Say or think to yourself the mantra *I Love*.

Exhale slowly. Bring your elbows together and round your back slightly. Your body does a subtle back bend as you inhale and a subtle forward bend as you exhale. Repeat as desired.

New Moon in Leo

How to Use the Moon Book With Your Chart

Fill in the blanks on the Cosmic Check-In page. Then look up the degree of the Moon on the chart below. Take note of the "I" statement on the outside of the wheel where the Moon is located. Now, locate the same degree on your own chart and make a note of the house and corresponding

"I" statement. Go back to the Cosmic Check-In page and circle the two statements from the charts and read what you wrote. This will give you an idea about what to expect from this moon phase on a personal level.

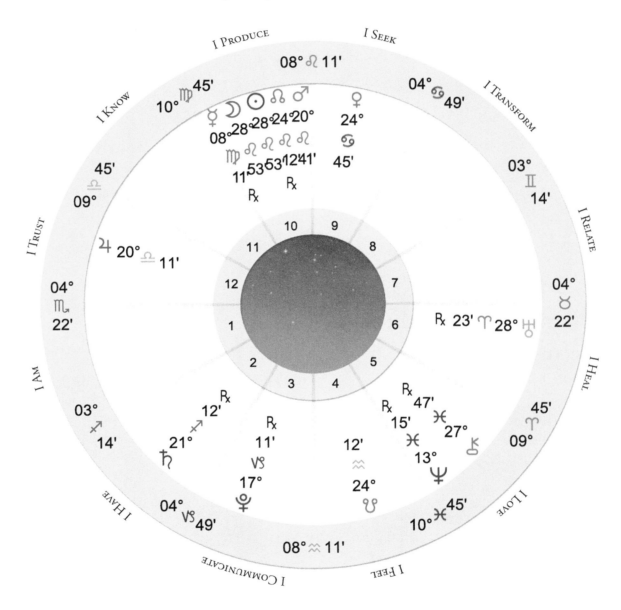

♈ Aries	♋ Cancer	♐ Sagittarius
♉ Taurus	♌ Leo	♑ Capricorn
♊ Gemini	♍ Virgo	♒ Aquarius
	♎ Libra	♓ Pisces
	♏ Scorpio	☉ Sun

☽ Moon	♄ Saturn	☊ North Node
☿ Mercury	♅ Uranus	☋ South Node
♀ Venus	♆ Neptune	➡ Enters
♂ Mars	♇ Pluto	℞ Retrograde
♃ Jupiter	⚷ Chiron	S/D Stationary Direct

V/C Void-of-Course
▲ Super-Sensitivity
▼ Low-Vitality

Cosmic Check-in

Take a moment to write a brief phrase for each "I" statement. This activates all areas of your life for this creative cycle.

♌ I Love

♍ I Heal

♎ I Relate

♏ I Transform

♐ I Seek

♑ I Produce

♒ I Know

♓ I Trust

♈ I Am

♉ I Have

♊ I Communicate

♋ I Feel

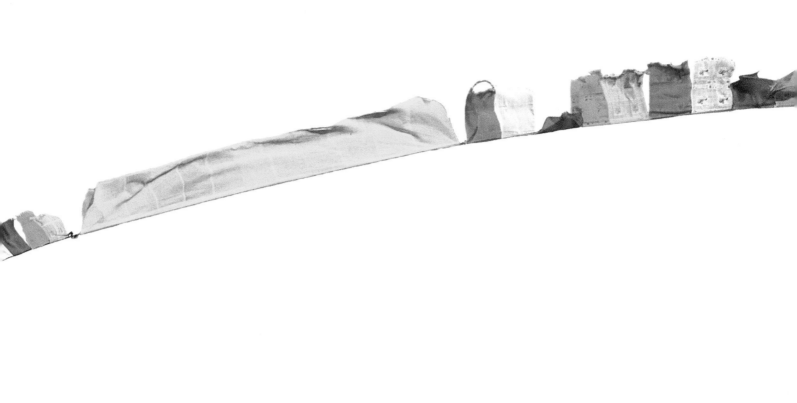

September

Planetary Highlights

Until September 5: Mercury retrograde in Leo

Take extra caution to not be misunderstood in love. Words and actions get confused if you prefer codependency over love.

Until September 28: Pluto retrograde in Capricorn

What is your personal survival issue? Is it money? Is it relationships? Is it staying physically fit? Jupiter and Uranus are extending our energetic boundaries, so know your baseline before this retrograde is over.

Until November 22: Neptune retrograde in Pisces

Pisces rules our path and Neptune rules our spiritual nature. Is your pathway in harmony with your spiritual development? To realign: breathe, meditate, and be in service to your community.

Until December 4: Chiron retrograde in Pisces

Reconcile your relationship with the spiritual world. Heal yourself and the whole world heals.

Until 2018: Uranus retrograde in Aries

It's hard to move forward without creating rebellion. Stop before trouble starts. What can you do to promote freedom in your life via the truth?

Until 2018: Jupiter in Libra opposite Uranus in Aries

Know your boundaries so you don't get stuck.

September 5: Mars enters Virgo

A new fitness program enchants you! If a new job has your name on it, change jobs.

September 9: Mercury enters Virgo

Virgo makes Mercury a happy messenger. Start a research project and pay attention to the divinity in the details!

September 13-14: Low Vitality

Allow things to end that have run their course. Get rest and know earth changes are possible.

September 19: Venus enters Virgo

If your self-esteem at work is challenged, you could suffer from perfectionism. Take time to play and all will be well.

September 19-25: Mars and Mercury coupled in Virgo

New knowledge is available, a dream come true for the mind. Let your brilliant mind shine and new discoveries will bring pleasure. Go fishing for details but don't lose sight of the pond.

September 22: Autumn Equinox—Sun enters Libra

As the days get shorter enjoy intimacy. Get close to each other as you turn inward during autumn.

September 27-28: Super Sensitivity

Stay out of the chaos that is in the air.

September 29: Mercury enters Libra

If your overactive mind is making you crazy, stop trying to figure things out. Trust your heart's understanding to guide you.

Sunday	Monday	Tuesday	Wednesday	Thursday	Friday	Saturday
					1 ☿♆♅♄♀♇℞ 6. Love dissolves judgement.	**2** ☿♆♅♄♀♇℞ ☽V/C 9:29AM ☽→♒ 1:06 PM 7. Think beyond the box and thrive.
3 ☿♆♅♄♀♇℞ 8. A leader creates prosperity for all.	**4** ☿♆♅♄♀♇℞ Labor Day ☽V/C 10:15 PM ☽→♓ 10:28 PM 9. Trust that the universe hears you.	**5** ☿♆♅♄♀♇℞ ☊☋-4:31AM 28°♌25′ ♂→♍ 2:36 AM 10. See your dream and live it now.	**6** ☿♆♅♄♀♇℞ ○13°♓53′ 12:02 AM ☽V/C 1:28PM 2. Who does your decision benefit?	**7** ♆♅♄♀♇℞ ☽→♈ 5:01 AM 3. Have fun, make everyone smile.	**8** ♆♅♄♀♇℞ 4. Develop a solid framework.	**9** ♆♅♄♀♇℞ ☽V/C 8:52 AM ☽→♉ 9:22 AM ☿→♍ 7:53 PM 5. Variety happens best by choice.
10 ♆♅♄♀♇℞ ☽V/C 5:54 PM 6. Romance is in the air, make it juicy.	**11** ♆♅♄♀♇℞ ☽→♊ 12:29 PM 7. Open your mind to a larger format.	**12** ♆♅♄♀♇℞ 8. Success is the result of application.	**13** ♆♅♄♀♇℞ ▼ ☽V/C 11:35 AM ☽→♋ 3:12 PM 9. Pray with a clear intent.	**14** ♆♅♄♀♇℞ ▼ 10. It's your choice to drop the past.	**15** ♆♅♄♀♇℞ ☽V/C 2:23 PM ☽→♌ 6:08 PM 2. Balance is achieved by action.	**16** ♆♅♄♀♇℞ 3. To play is more vital than to win.
17 ♆♅♄♀♇℞ ☽V/C 5:54 PM ☽→♍ 9:52 PM 4. Create order in a space that needs it.	**18** ♆♅♄♀♇℞ 5. Vary the way you cook tonight.	**19** ♆♅♄♀♇℞ ●27°♍27′ 10:29PM ☽V/C 10:29 PM ♀→♍ 6:16 PM 6. Light candles and play music.	**20** ♆♅♄♀♇℞ Rosh Hashanah ☽→♎ 3:05 AM 7. Be inspired, look for options.	**21** ♆♅♄♀♇℞ 8. Let generosity grace you today.	**22** ♆♅♄♀♇℞ ☽V/C 6:04 AM ☽→♏ 10:39 AM Autumn Equinox ☉→♎ 1:03 PM 9. Lend support to a humanitarian cause.	**23** ♆♅♄♀♇℞ 10. Buy something new for your love.
24 ♆♅♄♀♇℞ ☽V/C 12:32 AM ☽→♐ 9:00 PM 11. The Universe has no limits.	**25** ♆♅♄♀♇℞ 3. Do not take a defensive position.	**26** ♆♅♄♀♇℞ 4. Flexibility is forward movement.	**27** ♆♅♄♀♇℞ ▲ ☽V/C 4:08 AM ☽→♑ 9:24 AM 5. If the mind is foggy, take a walk.	**28** ♆♅♄♇℞ ▲ ☊☋-12:34PM 16°♑51′ 6. Tell someone you love them.	**29** ♆♅♄℞ Yom Kippur ☽V/C 5:13 AM ☽→♒ 9:40 PM ☿→♎ 5:43 PM 7. Knowledge is always changing.	**30** ♆♅♄℞ 8. Be grateful for your success.

♈ Aries	♎ Libra	☉ Sun	♄ Saturn	☊ North Node	▲ Super Sensitivity	6. Love
♉ Taurus	♏ Scorpio	☽ Moon	♅ Uranus	☋ South Node	▼ Low Vitality	7. Learning
♊ Gemini	♐ Sagittarius	☿ Mercury	♆ Neptune	→ Enters	2. Balance	8. Money
♋ Cancer	♑ Capricorn	♀ Venus	♇ Pluto	℞ Retrograde	3. Fun	9. Spirituality
♌ Leo	♒ Aquarius	♂ Mars	⚷ Chiron	S/D Stationary Direct	4. Structure	10. Visionary
♍ Virgo	♓ Pisces	♃ Jupiter		V/C Void-of-Course	5. Action	11. Completion

Full Moon in Pisces

September 6th, 12:02 AM

Statement I Trust
Body Feet
Mind Super-sensitive
Spirit Mystical
Element Water – Feeling, rhythm, living by cycles, flowing, and escaping from reality.

Degree Choice Points
13° Pisces 52'
Light Elegance
Shadow Glamour
Wisdom Remove the mask between you and the universe.

Tenth House Moon
1° Pisces 55'
Tenth House Umbrella Theme
I Produce/I Trust – Your approach to status, career, honor, and prestige, and why you chose your father.
Light Awareness
Shadow Invalidation
Wisdom An alternate reality helps you to adapt.

The Sun is Opposite the Moon

Full moons are always in opposition to the Sun. This creates a feeling of tension between where you want to shine and how your feelings are flowing on a sensory level about the Sun's directive. The two forces seem like they are working against each other, yet they are on the same team displaying different techniques to obtain the same mission. The Pisces/Virgo polarity creates tension between addiction and perfection.

Pisces Goddess

Lady Change'e, the Chinese Moon Goddess, is honored at the full moon closest to the Autumnal Equinox, with the sharing of moon cakes, whose round shape symbolizes completeness and togetherness. She ascended to the Moon after drinking the Elixir of Immortality. It had been gifted to her husband after he slew nine out of ten wayward sons of an emperor who had turned into suns and were scorching the Earth. If she and her husband had split the elixir, they would each be immortal, but her mistake in drinking it all (or her sacrifice, depending on the telling) means she will spend eternity on the Moon.

Depicted with a companion rabbit, a magical potion maker, Change'e is beneficent, and will grant your wishes, but remember she favors those who are careful what they wish for, and who take initiative towards working to make their own dreams a reality. Trust in the process of transformation, like the changing colors of the leaves, but also put both of your feet firmly on the path towards wholeness.

Build Your Altar

Colors Greens, blues, amethyst, aquamarine
Numerology 2 – Concentrate on wholeness
Tarot Card The Hanged Man – Learning to let go
Gemstones Opal, turquoise, amethyst
Plant remedy Passion flower – The ability to live in the here and now
Fragrance White lotus – Connecting to the Divine without arrogance

Clearing the Slate

Sixty hours before the full moon negative traits connected to the astro-sign might become activated to trigger what needs to be released during the full moon phase. You may notice a sudden urge to escape into unrealistic attitudes or addictive habits that bring a feeling of aimlessness. Make a list of the triggers and do Ho'oponopono, a Hawaiian Huna ritual for forgiveness. Look in the mirror, and for each negative trait, tell yourself *I am sorry, I forgive you, thank you for your awareness,* and *I love you.*

Pisces Victories and Challenges

Say all of the statements in this section out loud. Then, underline the phrase that means the most to you. Use the phrase as your special affirmation for recalibrating throughout this phase of the moon.

The best thing I can do for myself today is to get out of the way, so life can take its own course without the interference of my control drama. I take time out to let go and let things be. I have become too involved in the details and have lost sight of the vastness of the Universe, and the infinite possibilities that are available to me at all times and in every moment. I am aware that all I need is a different way of seeing what I have perceived as a problem, and that my view is limited by my needs, rather than by accepting things as they are. I trust that, when I get out of the way and give space to the power of NOW, all is in Divine Order and everything works out for the good of all concerned. This is the day when doing nothing gets me everything. I allow myself to experience the void. I empty myself of my rigidity, small-mindedness, racing thoughts, the need to be right, and to control outcomes. I know that non-action will present me with right action. I give the Universe a chance and trust the view to be larger than mine. When I accept myself as I am, I learn what I can become. I remove myself from all of the mind chatter and allow for silence to do its work. I am aware that a quiet mind brings me peace (the absence of conflict). In turning upside down, I see how right-side-up things really are. Acceptance brings me perspective. Acceptance sets me free. Acceptance brings me wholeness. Acceptance widens my mind.

Pisces Homework

Get a foot massage to bring your energy back to the ground. Feel the power of your path on the bottom of your feet. Now that you are back to your body, it is time to make a list of the ways your boundaries get breached. After the completion of your list, read it out loud and then throw it in the ocean.

Recalibrating List

I am a free spiritual being and it is my desire to be free to think and to express myself fully.

From this day forward I resolve to be true — first to myself and my highest self, and then to the highest self in me which is the Source of Love That I Am.

Pisces Recalibrating Ideas

Now is the time to activate a game change in my life, and give up addictions, illusions and fantasy, escape dramas, martyrdom, victimhood, and mental chaos.

Activate Acceleration

By acknowledging what you have recalibrated and overcome, you activate your acceleration. Keep this list active during this moon cycle.

Sky Power Yoga

Rocky Mountain Pose

No props are needed.

Stand with your feet hip-width apart. Lift your toes and wiggle them for 30 seconds. Spreading your toes wide, place them back on the floor.

As you exhale, rock back and forth and side to side—massaging the bottoms of your feet. Feel yourself grounded, stable, and strong amidst movement.

Settle into mountain pose. Squeeze your thighs to lift your kneecaps. Slightly tuck your tailbone down and feel your hips align over your ankles.

Lengthen your spine. Roll your shoulders back and down reaching your fingertips towards the floor. With your chest gently lifted from the sternum, turn your palms out slightly. To add support: imagine a strong line of vertical energy running from the bottom of your feet to the top of your head like a tree with strong roots running deep into the earth.

Relax. Close your eyes. Breathe in and out slowly and deeply several times through your nose with your awareness on your feet.

Inhale deeply as you say or think to yourself the mantra *I Trust.* As you exhale slowly, your exhalation roots you more deeply into the earth. Repeat as desired.

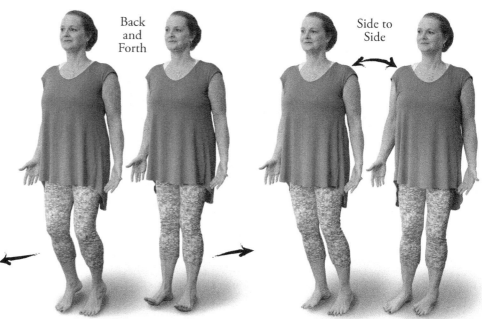

Back and Forth

Side to Side

Full Moon in Pisces

How to Use the Moon Book With Your Chart

Fill in the blanks on the Cosmic Check-In page. Then look up the degree of the Moon on the chart below. Take note of the "I" statement on the outside of the wheel where the Moon is located. Now, locate the same degree on your own chart and make a note of the house and corresponding

"I" statement. Go back to the Cosmic Check-In page and circle the two statements from the charts and read what you wrote. This will give you an idea about what to expect from this moon phase on a personal level.

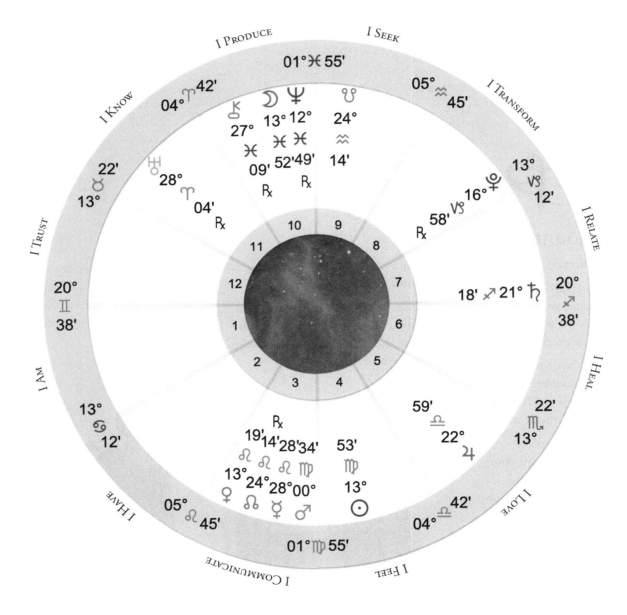

♈	Aries	♋	Cancer	♐	Sagittarius	☽	Moon	♄	Saturn	☊	North Node	V/C Void-of-Course
♉	Taurus	♌	Leo	♑	Capricorn	☿	Mercury	♅	Uranus	☋	South Node	▲ Super-Sensitivity
♊	Gemini	♍	Virgo	♒	Aquarius	♀	Venus	♆	Neptune	➡	Enters	▼ Low-Vitality
		♎	Libra	♓	Pisces	♂	Mars	♇	Pluto	℞	Retrograde	
		♏	Scorpio	☉	Sun	♃	Jupiter	⚷	Chiron	S/D	Stationary Direct	

Cosmic Check-in

Take a moment to write a brief phrase for each "I" statement. This activates all areas of your life for this creative cycle.

♓ I Trust

♈ I Am

♉ I Have

♊ I Communicate

♋ I Feel

♌ I Love

♍ I Heal

♎ I Relate

♏ I Transform

♐ I Seek

♑ I Produce

♒ I Know

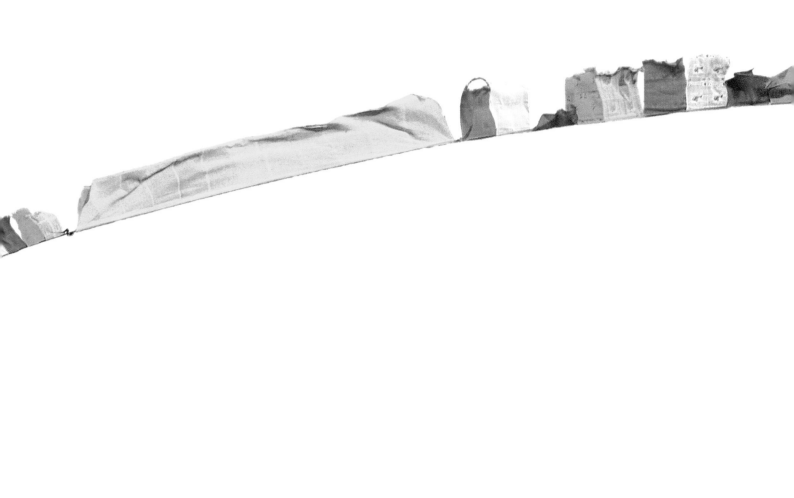

New Moon in Virgo

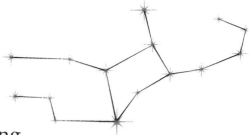

September 19th, 10:29 PM

Statement I Heal
Body Intestines
Mind Critical
Spirit Divinity in the Details
Element Earth – The way you manage your body and appearance. Family lineage and DNA healing, knowing abundance, healing power from the plant kingdom and nutrition, body awareness, and connection to small animals.

Degree Choice Points
27° Virgo 27'
Light "Take Charge" Ability
Shadow Power Tripping
Wisdom Withdraw your energy to prevent distortion.

Fifth House Moon
23° Virgo 16'

Fifth House Umbrella Theme
I Love/I Heal – The way you love and how you want to be loved.
Light Simplicity
Shadow Apathy
Wisdom Turn a project over to someone who can complete it.

Karmic Awakening

Karma is activated when there is a conflict between knowing and loving. If the expression of love inspires knowing, then all will be well. If your love is solid within yourself, then peer or group pressure will not challenge it.

When the Sun is in Virgo

Virgo is called the "Womb of Time" in which the seeds of great value are planted, shielded, nourished, and revealed. It is the labor of Virgo that brings the Christ Principle into manifestation within individuals and humanity. This unification occurs when we feel the power within us to serve. When we serve, we give birth to Divinity. Virgo time is when we all have a chance to raise the standard of excellence in our lives and on the Earth. The Virgo intelligence stores and maintains light in a precise manner. Attention to detail is Virgo's great gift to life.

Virgo Goddess

Mayan Goddess of medicine and midwifery, Ixchel, enters quietly in her jaguar form, to sit and observe. How are you being healed and how are you assisting the healing of others? Jaguar medicine is powerful for clearing attachments and cords that no longer serve you.

Call upon Ixchel to help you find precision and clarity through your words. Let her help you end negative self-talk. Enlist her to walk your boundaries and protect you fiercely, as though you were her little cub. Locate a stone or amulet you can carry in your pocket to remind you of her power, just like shaman and physicians of old would carry in their medicine bundles. When Ixchel has your back, you can roar!

Build Your Altar

Colors Earth tones, blue, green
Numerology 6 – Make romance a top priority
Tarot Card The Hermit – Being a shining light for all of life
Gemstones Emerald, malachite, sapphire
Plant Remedy Sagebrush – The ability to hold and store light
Fragrance Lavender – Management and storage of energy

Virgo Victories *and* Challenges

Say all of the statements in this section out loud. Then, underline the phrase that means the most to you. Use the phrase as your special affirmation for manifesting throughout this phase of the moon.

Today, I recognize what I love most about myself. I am the source of my love, my life, and my experience. I will set aside time today to nurture myself. I allow myself to receive these gifts and know in my heart that it is natural for me to love myself. I discover, deep within myself, the knowing that the love I give myself is commensurate to the love I am willing to receive from others. I am aware that what I expect from others cannot be truly expressed or experienced if I cannot give to myself first. I can never be disappointed when I know that love is a natural resource for me today.

Today, I honor the Earth by acknowledging what she has given me. I take time out to walk in the woods or on the beach, to feel the power of the creative pulse of the creative forces flowing through my body with the energy of being alive. I spend time in my garden and plant flowers to enhance the idea of beauty today. I honor my body today and get a massage. I spend quality time sharing joyful moments with those who love to connect from the heart and realize the blessings that come from living my life with love.

Virgo Homework

Virgos manifest best through working with herbology, folk medicine, environmental industries, organic farming, recycling, horticulture, acupuncture, healing arts, nutritional counseling, yoga instruction, and editing.

The Virgo moon cycle gives birth to Divinity in its own unique way, understanding the Soul's blueprint to be a temple of beauty. This creates what is known as the "crisis of perfection" within the minds of humankind during this time. We become aware of Spirit ascending and descending at the same time and must recognize that these contradicting energies are working within us in order to give birth to Divinity.

Manifesting List

This or something better than this comes to me in an easy and pleasurable way, for the good of all concerned. Thank you, Universe!

Virgo Manifesting Ideas

Now is the time to focus on manifesting a high standard of excellence, a healthy lifestyle, self-acceptance, discernment without judgment, healing abilities, a contribution to nature, and a healthy body.

Gratitude List

Keep this list active throughout the moon cycle. This will bring you to a level of completion so that a new cycle of opportunity can occur in your life. Be prepared for miracles!

Sky Power Yoga

Seated Spinal Twist

You need one chair for the prop.

With your back straight sit one hand-width from the back of the chair with your feet on the floor hip-width apart. If your feet require more solid contact with the floor, place pillows or folded towels under your feet.

Reach your right hand back to hold the chair just behind your sitting bones. Reach your left hand diagonally to cup the right knee.

While gazing forward, anchor your sitting bones into the chair. Then inhale and lengthen your spine.

Relax. Close your eyes. Breathe in and out slowly and deeply several times through your nose with your awareness on your intestines.

Inhale deeply as you say or think to yourself the mantra *I Heal.*

As you exhale softly, twist to turn your head towards your right shoulder using a subtle, gentle rotation. Feel your breath expanding your rib cage on the left side as well as massaging the spine and internal organs.

After several breaths, gently release the pose, return to facing forward, and repeat on the opposite side.

New Moon in Virgo

How to Use the Moon Book With Your Chart

Fill in the blanks on the Cosmic Check-In page. Then look up the degree of the Moon on the chart below. Take note of the "I" statement on the outside of the wheel where the Moon is located. Now, locate the same degree on your own chart and make a note of the house and corresponding

"I" statement. Go back to the Cosmic Check-In page and circle the two statements from the charts and read what you wrote. This will give you an idea about what to expect from this moon phase on a personal level.

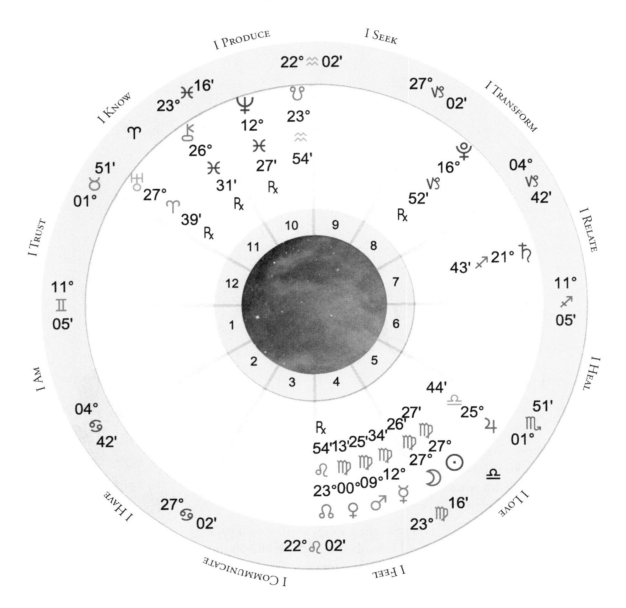

♈ Aries	♋ Cancer	♐ Sagittarius	☽ Moon	♄ Saturn	☊ North Node	V/C Void-of-Course
♉ Taurus	♌ Leo	♑ Capricorn	☿ Mercury	♅ Uranus	☋ South Node	▲ Super-Sensitivity
♊ Gemini	♍ Virgo	♒ Aquarius	♀ Venus	♆ Neptune	➡ Enters	▼ Low-Vitality
	♎ Libra	♓ Pisces	♂ Mars	♇ Pluto	℞ Retrograde	
	♏ Scorpio	☉ Sun	♃ Jupiter	⚷ Chiron	S/D Stationary Direct	

Cosmic Check-in

Take a moment to write a brief phrase for each "I" statement. This activates all areas of your life for this creative cycle.

♍ I Heal

♎ I Relate

♏ I Transform

♐ I Seek

♑ I Produce

♒ I Know

♓ I Trust

♈ I Am

♉ I Have

♊ I Communicate

♋ I Feel

♌ I Love

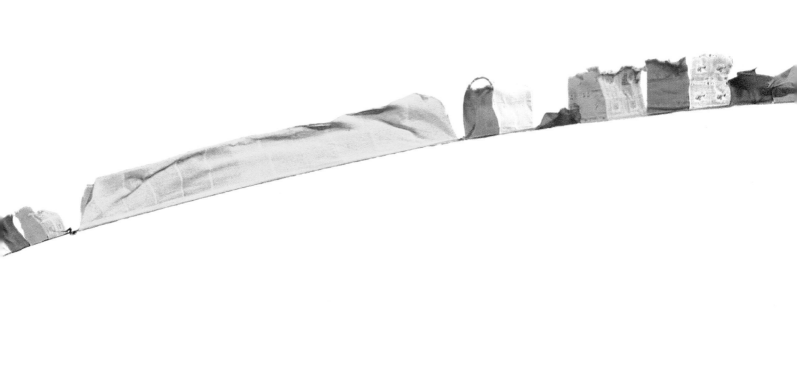

October

Planetary Highlights

Until 2018: Uranus retrograde in Aries

Recalibrate your identity by letting outdated aspects of your personality go. Your past identity is no longer current. Show the world the new you by updating your wardrobe.

Until November 22: Neptune retrograde in Pisces

Is your path winding in too many directions due to aimlessness? Get clear on your goals and free yourself from distractions.

Until December 4: Chiron retrograde in Pisces

To heal you must be willing to receive. Are your judgements blocking your ability to receive? Have you been suffering alone rather than asking for help?

October 1-9: Jupiter in Libra opposite Uranus in Aries

Jupiter and Uranus combine energies to add to our planet's quality of life. Use the power of acceleration to make the potential of this good fortune manifest.

October 1-10: Venus and Mars coupled in Virgo

Beware that you could get sex and love confused.

October 2-8: Sun and Mercury dance in Libra

High energy radiates through profound conversations. Share your glowing ideas with heart-to-heart friends as you fly together on a magic carpet ride through the sky.

October 10: Jupiter enters Scorpio

Jupiter rules your expansive nature and Scorpio rules your ability to share resources. Think big and abundance will flow your way as this configuration brings fortunes. How willing are you to share your abundance?

October 10-11: Low Vitality

Earth changes are possible—stay close to home.

October 14: Venus enters Libra

Breathe deeply the love that is in the air!

October 17: Mercury enters Scorpio

A fine-tuned focus on manifestation arrives into the mix of your life. Stay open to allow the alchemy of abundance to do its dance and live big!

October 22: Mars enters Libra

Diplomacy is the name of the game. Peace looks war in the eyes. Take the high road—avoid judgmental attitudes and use prayer instead.

October 22: Sun enters Scorpio

Face your shadow. How much have you placed under the carpet where money, sex, power, and death are concerned? If you bring your secrets to light, you recalibrate and transform your life closer to your essence.

October 24-25: Super Sensitivity

Recognize when you are mentally obsessing. Let go and all will be well.

Sunday	Monday	Tuesday	Wednesday	Thursday	Friday	Saturday
1 ♆♄♅℞ 9. Give thanks for all that you have.	**2** ♆♄♅℞ ☽V/C 4:12 AM ☽→♓ 7:26AM 10. Be clear with all your intentions.	**3** ♆♄♅℞ 2. Take action to stay in balance.	**4** ♆♄♅℞ ☽V/C 12:18 AM ☽→♈ 1:39PM 3. A playful attitude brings joy.	**5** ♆♄♅℞ ○ 12°♈43' 11:40AM 4. Trust the order of events.	**6** ♆♄♅℞ ☽V/C 3:37PM ☽→♉ 4:55PM 5. Make a difference by making a change.	**7** ♆♄♅℞ 6. Love is a principle not a practice.
8 ♆♄♅℞ ☽V/C 6:45AM ☽→♊ 6:44 PM 7. Clear thinking requires order.	**9** ♆♄♅℞ Columbus Day 8.Take charge, not control.	**10** ♆♄♅℞ ▼ ☽V/C 3:24 PM ☽→♋ 8:38 PM ♃→♏ 6:21AM 9. See yourself full-ing your dreams.	**11** ♆♄♅℞ ▼ 10. Create space for something new.	**12** ♆♄♅℞ ☽V/C 8:59PM ☽→♌ 11:41 PM 11. Remember you are part of the All.	**13** ♆♄♅℞ ☽V/C 10:27PM 3. Know that you are creative.	**14** ♆♄♅℞ ☽V/C 10:27PM ♀→♎ 3:12AM 4. To be in charge, stay flexible.
15 ♆♄♅℞ ☽→♍ 4:18 AM 5. Be willing to change as needed.	**16** ♆♄♅℞ 6. Let love renew itself daily.	**17** ♆♄♅℞ ☽V/C 4:26 AM ☽→♎ 9:34AM ☿→♏ 1:00 AM 7. Donate used books to a library.	**18** ♆♄♅℞ 8. Abundance comes in many forms.	**19** ♆♄♅℞ ● 26°♎35' 12:12PM ☽V/C 12:12 PM ☽→♏ 6:40 PM 9. Protect your spiritual wellbeing.	**20** ♆♄♅℞ 10. Starting over is a new beginning.	**21** ♆♄♅℞ 3. Be the best you can be in all you do.
22 ♆♄♅℞ ☽V/C 4:35 AM ☽→♐ 4:56 AM ♂→♎ 11:30AM ☉→♏ 10:28PM 4. Simplicity is key to staying on track.	**23** ♆♄♅℞ 5. Don't "try" to do it. Just do it.	**24** ♆♄♅℞ ▲ ☽V/C 9:44 AM ☽→♑ 5:12 PM 6. Listen to beautiful music.	**25** ♆♄♅℞ ▲ 7. Evaluate without judgment.	**26** ♆♄♅℞ ☽V/C 10:22PM 8. See challenge as opportunities.	**27** ♆♄♅℞ ☽→♒ 5:58AM 9. When you find a solution, be grateful.	**28** ♆♄♅℞ 10 Release the old to start the new.
29 ♆♄♅℞ ☽V/C 9:21 AM ☽→♓ 4:46 PM 11. Connect with the Universal flow.	**30** ♆♄♅℞ 3. Own that life is playful and joyful.	**31** ♆♄♅℞ Halloween ☽V/C 2:07PM ☽→♈ 11:42 PM 4. Organize by eliminating.				

♈ Aries	♎ Libra	☉ Sun	♄ Saturn	☊ North Node	▲ Super Sensitivity	6. Love
♉ Taurus	♏ Scorpio	☽ Moon	♅ Uranus	☋ South Node	▼ Low Vitality	7. Learning
♊ Gemini	♐ Sagittarius	☿ Mercury	♆ Neptune	➡ Enters	2. Balance	8. Money
♋ Cancer	♑ Capricorn	♀ Venus	♇ Pluto	℞ Retrograde	3. Fun	9. Spirituality
♌ Leo	♒ Aquarius	♂ Mars	⚷ Chiron	S/D Stationary Direct	4. Structure	10. Visionary
♍ Virgo	♓ Pisces	♃ Jupiter		V/C Void-of-Course	5. Action	11. Completion

Full Moon in Aries

October 5th, 11:40 AM

Statement I Am
Body Head and Face
Mind Ego
Spirit Awakening
Element Fire – Inspiration, action, initiation, passion, enthusiasm, "it's my way or the high way," and the divine masculine.

Degree Choice Points
12° Aries 43'
Light Diffusion
Shadow Subservience
Wisdom Accept your angelic roots.

Fourth House Moon
27° Pisces 15'
Fourth House Umbrella Theme
I Feel/I Trust – How your early environmental training was, how that set your foundation for living, and why you chose your mother.
Light Wisdom's Rewards
Shadow Possessiveness
Wisdom Appreciate your body's intelligence.

The Sun is Opposite the Moon

Full moons are always in opposition to the Sun. This creates a feeling of tension between where you want to shine and how your feelings are flowing on a sensory level about the Sun's directive. The two forces seem like they are working against each other, yet they are on the same team displaying different techniques to obtain the same mission. The Aries/Libra polarity creates tension between "I Am" and "We Are".

Aries Goddess

Heqet, the Fertility Goddess of the early dynastic period of Egypt, is often depicted on the amulets of pregnant women as a frog sitting on a lotus. Associated with germination of corn following the flooding of the Nile (when frogs were most prolific), and with the final stages of childbirth, she is said to breathe the "breath of life" into the bodies of newborn children who are formed on the potter's wheel of her partner Khnum. It was she who breathed life into Horus, in the myth of Isis and Osiris.

The moonlight is now shining on you as you take your self-confidence and self-awareness to a new level. Is it time for you to take on a new role within your community? Have you developed new knowledge, skills, and qualities that you're ready to try out? Ask Heqet to assist you through the stages from tadpole to adult, as you lose your tail and develop your sea legs.

Build Your Altar

Colors Red, black, coral
Numerology 4 – Trust the order of events
Tarot Card Tower – Release from a stuck place, a major breakthrough
Gemstones Diamond, red jasper, coral, obsidian
Plant remedy Oak, pomegranate – Planting new life and rooting new life
Fragrance Ginger – The ability to ingest and digest life

Clearing the Slate

Aries Full Moon
October 5th
11:40 AM

Sixty hours before the full moon negative traits connected to the astro-sign might become activated to trigger what needs to be released during the full moon phase. You may notice a sudden need to be first or impatience that could lead to anger or arrogance. Make a list of the triggers and do Ho'oponopono, a Hawaiian Huna ritual for forgiveness. Look in the mirror, and for each negative trait, tell yourself *I am sorry, I forgive you, thank you for your awareness,* and *I love you.*

Aries Victories and Challenges

Say all of the statements in this section out loud. Then, underline the phrase that means the most to you. Use the phrase as your special affirmation for recalibrating throughout this phase of the moon.

Today, I let go. I trust that whatever breaks down or breaks through is a blessing in disguise for me. I make a commitment to allow myself to be spontaneous and live in the moment. I know the unexpected is a blessing for me and a way for me to make a breakthrough out of my limitations. I am aware that I am resistant to change. I know I must make changes and am too stubborn to take the appropriate action myself to change. I have built many walls of false protection around me, guarding me and blocking me from the reality that change is a constant. I have freeze-framed my life and desire support to update myself. I have allowed my fear of change to become my false motto and my life is at a standstill. I am unwilling to use any more energy to perpetuate my resistance. I know that continuing to cling to the past is a waste of my energy. I can no longer put things off that delay my process. I feel the breaking down of form. I trust that all changes are in my favor. All changes lead me to golden opportunities. I release false pride. I release false foundations. I release false authorities. In so doing, I allow for everything to crumble around me so I can see that my true strength is within and I will build my life from the inside out.

I am ready for new experiences. I am ready for the unexpected. I am willing to have an event occur so I can become activated towards my breakthrough. I am ready for the power of now. I know being spontaneous will bring me to true joy. I know if I ride this carrier wave it will take me to a place far beyond my scope of limited thinking. I know the will of God works in my favor and knows more than I do in any given moment.

Aries Homework

Now you are ready to take a personal inventory on behaviors such as impatience, talking over people, brat attacks, and starting every sentence with "I."

This is a time when the light becomes a prisoner of polarized forces. This diminishing light begins its yearly sojourn beneath the surface, asking us to balance light and dark by mastering the concept of equilibrium. Equilibrium is the Law of Harmony, where we attempt to reach a state of achievement by combining paradoxical fields that break the crystallization of polarity. Spend time looking for increasing and decreasing fields of light around you.

Recalibrating List

Say this statement out loud three times before writing your recalibrating list:

I am a free spiritual being and it is my desire to be free to think and to express myself fully.

From this day forward I resolve to be true – first to myself and my highest self, and then to the highest self in me which is the Source of Love That I Am.

Aries Recalibrating Ideas

Now is the time to activate a game change in my life, and give up anger as a default, competition and comparison, irritation and struggle, the need to be first, overdoing it and not resting, impatience, impulsiveness, and hostility.

Activate Acceleration

By acknowledging what you have recalibrated and overcome, you activate your acceleration. Keep this list active during this moon cycle.

Sky Power Yoga

Resting Pose

You need one pillow and one blanket for the prop.

Lie on your back with your legs spread shoulder-width apart. Place your arms by your side at a 45-degree angle with your palms facing down. You may place a pillow under your neck for support or cover yourself with a blanket to stay warm.

Relax. Close your eyes. Breathe in and out slowly and deeply several times through your nose with your awareness on your head. Allow your body to soften and relax until it feels like you are melting into the floor.

Feel the gentle rhythmic massage of the body as your belly subtly rises and falls with each breath. Allow this awareness to increase your sense of being grounded and supported.

Inhale and envision the energy of your breath coming up from the earth into your feet and then up your legs, your spine, and out the top of your head. Say or think to yourself the mantra *I Am.*

Exhale softly and slowly as you envision your breath flowing back into your head and down your spine, your legs, and out your feet back into the earth. Repeat as desired.

Full Moon in Aries

How to Use the Moon Book With Your Chart

Fill in the blanks on the Cosmic Check-In page. Then look up the degree of the Moon on the chart below. Take note of the "I" statement on the outside of the wheel where the Moon is located. Now, locate the same degree on your own chart and make a note of the house and corresponding

"I" statement. Go back to the Cosmic Check-In page and circle the two statements from the charts and read what you wrote. This will give you an idea about what to expect from this moon phase on a personal level.

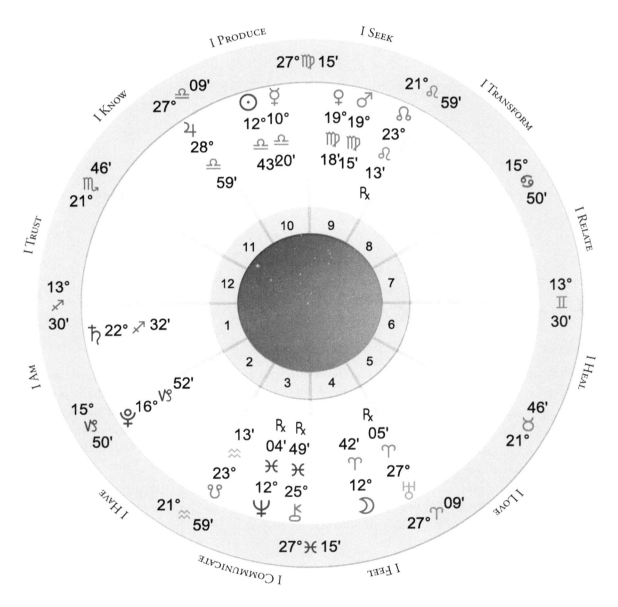

♈	Aries	♋	Cancer	♐	Sagittarius	☽	Moon	♄	Saturn	☊	North Node	V/C Void-of-Course
♉	Taurus	♌	Leo	♑	Capricorn	☿	Mercury	♅	Uranus	☋	South Node	▲ Super-Sensitivity
♊	Gemini	♍	Virgo	♒	Aquarius	♀	Venus	♆	Neptune	➡	Enters	▼ Low-Vitality
		♎	Libra	♓	Pisces	♂	Mars	♇	Pluto	℞	Retrograde	
		♏	Scorpio	☉	Sun	♃	Jupiter	⚷	Chiron	S/D	Stationary Direct	

Cosmic Check-in

Take a moment to write a brief phrase for each "I" statement. This activates all areas of your life for this creative cycle.

♈ I Am

♉ I Have

♊ I Communicate

♋ I Feel

♌ I Love

♍ I Heal

♎ I Relate

♏ I Transform

♐ I Seek

♑ I Produce

♒ I Know

♓ I Trust

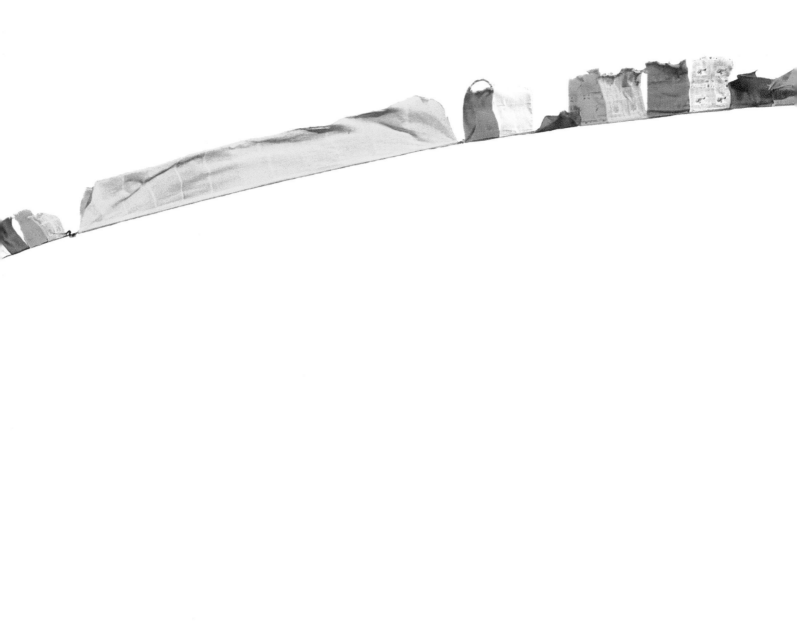

New Moon in Libra

Statement I Relate

Body Kidneys

Mind Social

Spirit Peace

Element Air – Promotes curiosity, insights, fresh perspectives, and bridges the Divine and the mundane.

Degree Choice Points
26° Libra 35'

Light Power of Love

Shadow Conflicting Actions

Wisdom Extra-planetary experiences enter your life when you defragment.

Tenth House Moon
20° Libra 53'

Tenth House Umbrella Theme
I Produce/I Relate – Your approach to status, career, honor, and prestige, and why you chose your father.

Light Social Participation

Shadow Disengagement

Wisdom Honesty and receptivity don't require analysis.

When the Sun is in Libra

Libra energy gives us the opportunity to bridge the gap between the higher and lower mind; abstract thinking versus concrete thinking. During Libra time, the light and dark forces are in balance and you are given a chance to experience harmony. Harmony occurs when you keep your polarities in motion and put paradox to rest, thus breaking the crystallization of polarity. Now is the time to weigh your values through the light of your Soul. Libra asks you to look at what is increasing and decreasing in your life. Start with friendship, courage, sincerity, and understanding, and keep going until your scale is in motion.

Libra Goddess

The Black Madonna, is a goddess archetype found all over the world, in her many associations as Isis, Mary Magdalene, Sara, Kali, or Virgin of Guadalupe. She offers up compassion and understanding for the human condition. Black is all colors, completely absorbed, and in her blackness she encompasses all and gives solace and miracles to any seeking comfort. Often depicted with a child in arms, a halo or ring of stars around her head, and a moon at her feet, the Black Madonna is the protectress of those who are marginalized. She is connected seamlessly to Heaven and Earth, as a fully incarnated woman and mother who has known deep sorrow, passion, joy, and love.

Grant her real life experience equal weight with the images of virginal perfection offered up as ideal, and she will help you have compassion for yourself and others experiencing the struggle of living and relating.

Build Your Altar

Colors Pink, green

Numerology 9 – Protect your spiritual wellbeing

Tarot Card Justice – The Law of Cause and Effect

Gemstones Jade, rose quartz

Plant Remedy Olive trees – Stamina

Fragrance Eucalyptus – Clarity of breath

Libra Victories *and* Challenges

Say all of the statements in this section out loud. Then, underline the phrase that means the most to you. Use the phrase as your special affirmation for manifesting throughout this phase of the moon.

I feel the call of the higher worlds awakening me to a new vibration. This call is to move beyond judgment and move to a place of acceptance, understanding, unconditional confidence, and love. I am at a place in my life where I can embrace the world of acceptance and wholeness, because I have birthed myself anew, beyond the imprisonment and crystallization of polarity and righteousness. My black and white worlds of right and wrong have integrated and blended into gray, the color of wisdom, where true knowledge exists. Knowledge simply is, and the need for proof does not exist where wisdom lives.

The only requirement is experience. I know that everything that comes before me is a direct reflection of my own experience and, in embracing this concept, I can now receive the gift of infinite awareness. I am in a place of awareness that came before and goes beyond where good and evil exist. I have within me, the presence of unconditional confidence to go where true love lives. I no longer need to prove myself.

I am now simply being myself. I release the need to be right and accept the right to BE. I no longer need to be forgiven, because I am neither wrong nor right. I no longer need to define myself. Acceptance has no reason for defense. I no longer need to be guilty; duty motivation is no longer a reality. I know that where there is judgment, there is separation. I know understanding unifies. I accept the call of the higher worlds and express myself freely and fully without fear of judgment. I accept myself as I am, so I can learn what I can become.

Libra Homework

Libras manifest best through the legal industry, beauty industry, diplomatic service, match-making, urban development, mediation, feng shui, spa ownership, clutter-busting and space clearing, romance writing, wedding consulting, fashion design, and as librarians.

It is time to weigh and measure the values of relationship, friendship, courage, sensitivity, sincerity, and understanding. Look at what is increasing and what is decreasing in these areas.

Manifesting List

This or something better than this comes to me in an easy and pleasurable way, for the good of all concerned. Thank you, Universe!

Libra Manifesting Ideas

Now is the time to focus on manifesting relationships, wholeness, being loving, lovable, and loved, living life as an art form, balance and equality, integrity, accuracy, diplomacy, and peace.

Gratitude List

Keep this list active throughout the moon cycle. This will bring you to a level of completion so that a new cycle of opportunity can occur in your life. Be prepared for miracles!

Sky Power Yoga

Seated Forward Fold

You need one chair for the prop.

With your back straight sit one hand-width from the back of the chair with your feet on the floor hip-width apart. If your feet require more solid contact with the floor, place pillows or folded towels under your feet.

Place hands on thighs just above knees. While gazing forward, anchor your sitting bones into the chair. Then inhale and lengthen your spine and neck towards the ceiling.

Relax. Close your eyes. Breathe in and out slowly and deeply several times through your nose with your awareness on your kidneys.

Inhale softly as you say or think to yourself the mantra *I Relate*. Exhale slowly, hinging at the hips with a straight back (hands slide forward over knees and down shins towards the floor). Stop once you feel any tightness in the back of your legs.

Release the neck and drop your head slightly. Inhale and exhale in this position for a few breaths.

Bring your head back to neutral in line with the spine, engage your abdominals, straighten your spine and return to sitting upright facing forward. Repeat as desired.

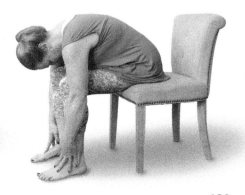

189

New Moon in Libra

How to Use the Moon Book With Your Chart

Fill in the blanks on the Cosmic Check-In page. Then look up the degree of the Moon on the chart below. Take note of the "I" statement on the outside of the wheel where the Moon is located. Now, locate the same degree on your own chart and make a note of the house and corresponding

"I" statement. Go back to the Cosmic Check-In page and circle the two statements from the charts and read what you wrote. This will give you an idea about what to expect from this moon phase on a personal level.

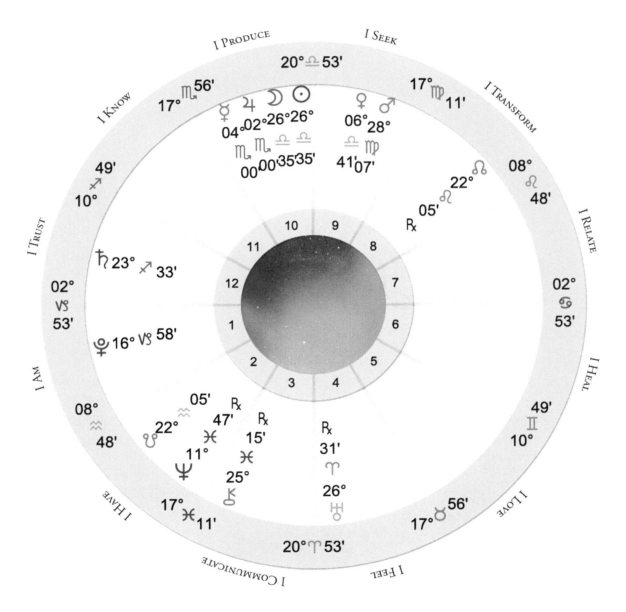

♈ Aries	♋ Cancer	♐ Sagittarius	☽ Moon	♄ Saturn	☊ North Node	V/C Void-of-Course
♉ Taurus	♌ Leo	♑ Capricorn	☿ Mercury	♅ Uranus	☋ South Node	▲ Super-Sensitivity
♊ Gemini	♍ Virgo	♒ Aquarius	♀ Venus	♆ Neptune	➡ Enters	▼ Low-Vitality
	♎ Libra	♓ Pisces	♂ Mars	♇ Pluto	℞ Retrograde	
	♏ Scorpio	☉ Sun	♃ Jupiter	⚷ Chiron	⬠ Stationary Direct	

Cosmic Check-in

Take a moment to write a brief phrase for each "I" statement. This activates all areas of your life for this creative cycle.

♎ I Relate

♏ I Transform

♐ I Seek

♑ I Produce

♒ I Know

♓ I Trust

♈ I Am

♉ I Have

♊ I Communicate

♋ I Feel

♌ I Love

♍ I Heal

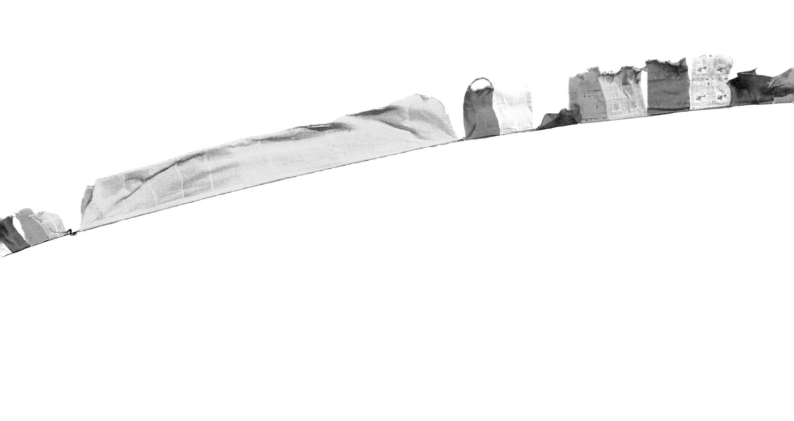

November

Planetary Highlights

Until November 22: Neptune retrograde in Pisces

Recalibrate your broken dreams into new inspirational insights. Don't be a martyr or a victim.

Until December 4: Chiron retrograde in Pisces

Chiron teaches that we don't have pain if we live in the present. Past hurts linger when silenced. Connect with your pain-body and ask what it wants you to hear. Listen and let healing begin.

Until 2018: Uranus retrograde in Aries

Pay attention as everything is changing. Get out of the way and allow new innovative trends to inspire new beginnings in your life.

November 3: Sun coupled with Jupiter

Let your intentions manifest—especially those related to abundance. May all your wishes be spontaneously fulfilled!

November 3-5: Venus in Libra opposite Uranus in Aries

"I" or "we"—which will it be? Work on your relationships by meditating on this amazing polarity.

November 7: Venus enters Scorpio

Prepare for the best sex you can imagine. Dance the dance of life and go deep.

November 7-8: Low Vitality

Get rest.

November 21: Sun enters Sagittarius

Celebrate! Adventure is in the air! Plan a trip or welcome in a new ritual for spiritual awakening.

November 18-21: Jupiter coupled with Venus in Scorpio

The art of living love becomes a reality. A week to remember for the rest of your life! Unconditional love and conditional love meet up to transform your love equation. Live fully, love fully, and enjoy deeply satisfying sex and other arts.

November 20-21 and 29-30: Super Sensitivity

The mental world creates confusion in your life if you allow it. Use your power of knowing, rather than thinking.

Sunday	Monday	Tuesday	Wednesday	Thursday	Friday	Saturday
			1 ⚷♆♅☋℞ 5. Be willing to be curious.	**2** ⚷♆♅☋℞ ☽V/C 8:02 PM 6. Always come from your heart.	**3** ⚷♆♅☋℞ ○ 11°♉59′ 10:22 PM ☽→♉ 2:46 AM 7. Clarify your ideas and move forward.	**4** ⚷♆♅☋℞ 8. Rely on yourself to manifest.
5 ⚷♆♅☋℞ PST Begins ☽V/C 1:28 AM ☽→♊ 2:26 AM ☿→♐ 11:20 AM 9. Focus on your spiritual goals.	**6** ⚷♆♅☋℞ 10. You can transform in a blink.	**7** ⚷♆♅☋℞ ▼ ☽V/C 2:39 AM ☽→♋ 2:44 AM ♀→♏ 3:40AM 11. The Universe always provides.	**8** ⚷♆♅☋℞ ▼ ☽V/C 9:14 PM 3. Have the ability to laugh at yourself.	**9** ⚷♆♅☋℞ ☽→♌ 4:29 AM 4. To be prepared is to be organized.	**10** ⚷♆♅☋℞ 5. Remember you activate change.	**11** ⚷♆♅☋℞ Veterans Day ☽V/C 12:55 AM ☽→♍ 8:41 AM 6. A wonderful gift is a smile.
12 ⚷♆♅☋℞ 7. Keep your thinking process flexible.	**13** ⚷♆♅☋℞ ☽V/C 7:45 AM ☽→♎ 3:26 PM 8. Be willing to share your wealth.	**14** ⚷♆♅☋℞ 9. Remember to stay spiritually awake.	**15** ⚷♆♅☋℞ ☽V/C 4:50 PM 10. Integrate a new technology.	**16** ⚷♆♅☋℞ ☽→♏ 12:18 AM 11. Be willing to add whatever is needed.	**17** ⚷♆♅☋℞ 3. Don't take yourself so seriously.	**18** ⚷♆♅☋℞ ● 26°♏19′ 3:42AM ☽V/C 3:42 AM ☽→♐ 10:58 AM 4. Even bridges need firm foundations.
19 ⚷♆♅☋℞ 5. Help a friend in necessary changes.	**20** ⚷♆♅☋℞ ▲ ☽V/C 4:26 PM ☽→♑ 11:14 PM 6. Sincerity comes from the heart.	**21** ⚷♆♅☋℞ ▲ ☉→♐ 7:06PM 7. A flexible mind is Divinely directed.	**22** ⚷♅☋℞ ♆ S/D 11°♓28′ 6:22AM 8. Pure intention = manifestation.	**23** ⚷♅☋℞ Thanksgiving Day ☽V/C 2:32 AM ☽→♒ 12:14 PM 9. Helping others is a spiritual exercise.	**24** ⚷♅☋℞ 10. A bright tomorrow begins today.	**25** ⚷♅☋℞ ☽VOC 6:36 PM 11. Choose to flow with grace and ease.
26 ⚷♅☋℞ ☽→♓ 12:03 AM 3. A sense of humor works wonders.	**27** ⚷♅☋℞ 4. Be sure to use all the parts.	**28** ⚷♅☋℞ ☽V/C 4:08 AM ☽→♈ 8:30 AM 5. Stop repeating the same old thing.	**29** ⚷♅☋℞ ▲ 6. Bring love into life.	**30** ⚷♅☋℞ ▲ ☽V/C 10:37 AM ☽→♉ 12:38 PM 7. Don't think, use the thought.		

♈ Aries	♎ Libra	☉ Sun	♄ Saturn	☊ North Node	▲ Super Sensitivity	6. Love
♉ Taurus	♏ Scorpio	☽ Moon	♅ Uranus	☋ South Node	▼ Low Vitality	7. Learning
♊ Gemini	♐ Sagittarius	☿ Mercury	♆ Neptune	➡ Enters	2. Balance	8. Money
♋ Cancer	♑ Capricorn	♀ Venus	♇ Pluto	℞ Retrograde	3. Fun	9. Spirituality
♌ Leo	♒ Aquarius	♂ Mars	⚷ Chiron	S/D Stationary Direct	4. Structure	10. Visionary
♍ Virgo	♓ Pisces	♃ Jupiter		V/C Void-of-Course	5. Action	11. Completion

Full Moon in Taurus

November 3rd, 10:22 PM

Statement I Have
Body Neck
Mind Collector
Spirit Accumulation
Element Earth – Self-value, abundance, aesthetics, business, sensuality, art, beauty, flowers, gardens, the collector, and the shopper.

Degree Choice Points
11° Taurus 59'
Light Shared Dreams
Shadow Consumerism
Wisdom Receive cosmic knowledge.
Tenth House Moon
7° Aries 37'
Tenth House Umbrella Theme
I Produce/I Am – Your approach to status, career, honor, and prestige, and why you chose your father.
Light Guided by Spirit
Shadow Posing
Wisdom Everything is experience—there is no positive or negative.

The Sun is Opposite the Moon

Full moons are always in opposition to the Sun. This creates a feeling of tension between where you want to shine and how your feelings are flowing on a sensory level about the Sun's directive. The two forces seem like they are working against each other, yet they are on the same team displaying different techniques to obtain the same mission. The Taurus/Scorpio polarity creates tension between "my" money and "our" money.

Taurus Goddess

The Roman Goddess of Abundance and Opportunity, Copia, invites you to drink deeply from her overflowing horn of plenty. As you harvest the bounties of your desires from the seeds you planted last Spring, thank Copia for the increase in your abundance factor! There is no greater prayer than the act of giving thanks.

During this Taurus moon, let receptivity and gratitude be in your attitude and actions! With open hands and heart, ask for Copia's presence at your table, and allow her to fill your cup with blessings. Encourage your gratitude to expand and generously influence all with whom you interact.

Build Your Altar

Colors Scarlet, earth tones
Numerology 7 – Clarify your ideas and move forward
Tarot Card Hierophant – Spiritual authority
Gemstones Red coral, red agate, garnet
Plant remedy Angelica – Connecting Heaven and Earth
Fragrance Rose – Opening the heart

Clearing the Slate

Sixty hours before the full moon negative traits connected to the astro-sign might become activated to trigger what needs to be released during the full moon phase. You may notice a sudden unwillingness to share or find yourself being stubborn, wasteful, or resisting change. Make a list of the triggers and do Ho'oponopono, a Hawaiian Huna ritual for forgiveness. Look in the mirror, and for each negative trait, tell yourself *I am sorry, I forgive you, thank you for your awareness,* and *I love you.*

Taurus Victories and Challenges

Say all of the statements in this section out loud. Then, underline the phrase that means the most to you. Use the phrase as your special affirmation for manifesting throughout this phase of the moon.

Everything is possible for me today. My possibilities are endless. I have the power within me to make all of my dreams come true. I have the tools to make my talent a reality. I have the power to identify with my talent. Today, I focus my attention and intention on manifesting with my talent and, in so doing, I transform my ideas into reality. I recognize the part of me that is connected to the cosmic source of ideas and I express that source within me to manifest my creative power. I see my possibilities and act on them today. I am the creative power. I am all-knowing. I am an individual. There is no one else like me. I can manifest anything I desire. I intend it, I allow it, so be it.

Rules for Manifesting

Know what you want. Write it down. Say it out loud. Recognize that because you thought it, it can be so. Release your limiting beliefs. Override your limiting beliefs with power statements. Act as if you have already manifested your idea. Lastly, value yourself!

Taurus Homework

Taureans manifest best when buying, selling, and owning real estate, gardening and landscaping, selling and collecting art, manufacturing and selling fine furniture, singing or acting, and as a restaurateur, antique dealer, or interior designer.

The Taurus moon asks us to infuse light into form and, in so doing, the bridge between humanity and divinity is actualized and we can assume our stewardship in the physical world. When we release Spirit into matter, we become open to the idea that accumulation and actualization set us free to experience the abundance available to us here on Earth. Go shopping!

Recalibrating List

Say this statement out loud three times before writing your recalibrating list:

I am a free spiritual being and it is my desire to be free to think and to express myself fully.

From this day forward I resolve to be true — first to myself and my highest self, and then to the highest self in me which is the Source of Love That I Am.

Taurus Recalibrating Ideas

Now is the time to activate a game change in my life, and give up envy, financial insecurity, being stubborn, hoarding, addictive spending, not feeling valuable, and fear of change.

Activate Acceleration

By acknowledging what you have recalibrated and overcome, you activate your acceleration. Keep this list active during this moon cycle.

Sky Power Yoga

Seated Fish

You need one chair for the prop.

With your back straight sit one hand-width from the back of the chair with your feet on the floor hip-width apart. If your feet require more solid contact with the floor, place pillows or folded towels under your feet.

Place hands on the sides of the chair with elbows pulled in slightly and pointing towards the chair back. Gently lift your chest from the sternum with your head and neck remaining neutral.

Relax. Close your eyes. Breathe in and out slowly and deeply several times through your nose with your awareness on your neck.

Inhale softly as you say or think to yourself the mantra *I Have.* Tilt the chin upward slightly as you envision the energy of mantra in your throat. Remain for three breaths.

On the next exhale, softly and slowly release the chin and the elbows. Ground your breath and the mantra into the earth as you release the pose. Repeat as desired.

Full Moon in Taurus

How to Use the Moon Book With Your Chart

Fill in the blanks on the Cosmic Check-In page. Then look up the degree of the Moon on the chart below. Take note of the "I" statement on the outside of the wheel where the Moon is located. Now, locate the same degree on your own chart and make a note of the house and corresponding

"I" statement. Go back to the Cosmic Check-In page and circle the two statements from the charts and read what you wrote. This will give you an idea about what to expect from this moon phase on a personal level.

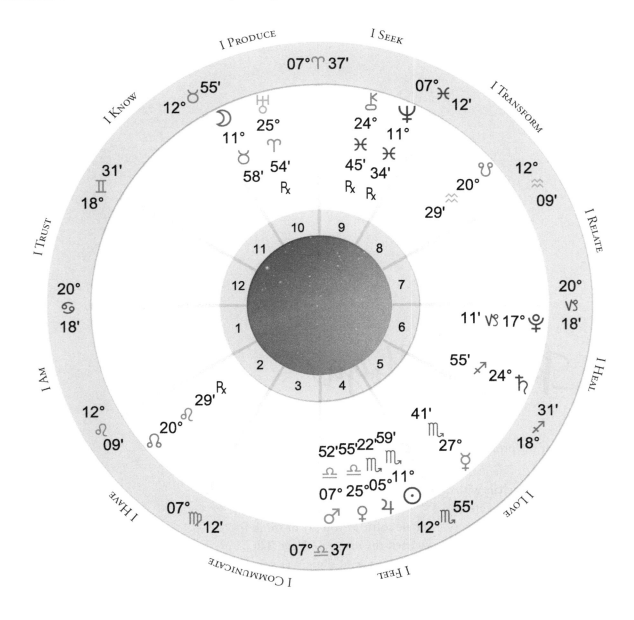

♈	Aries	♋	Cancer	♐	Sagittarius	☽	Moon	♄	Saturn	☊	North Node	V/C Void-of-Course
♉	Taurus	♌	Leo	♑	Capricorn	☿	Mercury	♅	Uranus	☋	South Node	▲ Super-Sensitivity
♊	Gemini	♍	Virgo	♒	Aquarius	♀	Venus	♆	Neptune	→	Enters	▼ Low-Vitality
		♎	Libra	♓	Pisces	♂	Mars	♇	Pluto	℞	Retrograde	
		♏	Scorpio	☉	Sun	♃	Jupiter	⚷	Chiron	S/D	Stationary Direct	

Cosmic Check-in

Take a moment to write a brief phrase for each "I" statement. This activates all areas of your life for this creative cycle.

♉ I Have

♊ I Communicate

♋ I Feel

♌ I Love

♍ I Heal

♎ I Relate

♏ I Transform

♐ I Seek

♑ I Produce

♒ I Know

♓ I Trust

♈ I Am

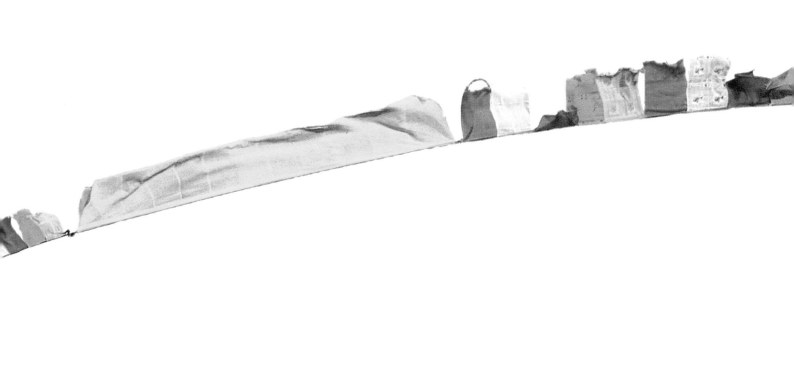

New Moon in Scorpio

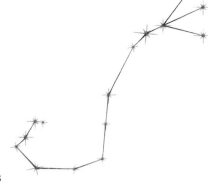

November 18th, 3:42 AM

Statement I Transform

Body Reproductive Organs

Mind Investigation

Spirit Transformation

Element Water -- Intense, passionate, sexual, powerful, focused, controlling, deep, driven, and secretive.

Degree Choice Points
26° Scorpio 19'

Light Authoritative Power

Shadow Audacity

Wisdom Use discernment within any relationship.

Second House Moon
20° Scorpio 31'

Second House Umbrella Theme
I Have/I Transform – The way you make your money and the way you spend it.

Light Conscientious Objection

Shadow Anarchy

Wisdom Be true to yourself through genuine self-expression.

When the Sun is in Scorpio

Scorpio is the symbol of darkness which heralds the decline of the Sun in Autumn. Scorpio embodies the Law of Nature, which decrees that even the strongest will must bow to the body's mortality. As we watch all of nature going through a slow death, we begin to recognize the qualities of Scorpio's subtlety and depth, and the hidden forces that threaten those who live only on the surface. Scorpio rules all of the things that you try to keep hidden: death, taxes, power, money, sex, resentment, revenge, ambition, pride, and fear. When you face these self-imposed limits on yourself, you take on the true power of transformation. Transformation establishes pathways for you to decentralize the ego in the interest of higher humanitarian work.

Scorpio Goddess

Scorpio moons ask you to delve deep into your Soul. There's no better companion in this process than Inanna, who journeyed to the Underworld and relinquished her power and possessions, one-at-a-time at each of seven gates, until she was stripped bare to her essential self, without any trappings or embellishments.

Ask your soul sister Inanna to accompany you in a candle-lit meditation to release that which you no longer need to carry in each of your seven chakras. Let go of anything encumbering your essential self, anything weighing you down. Connect with the dark, cool Earth and tune into anything that you feel like you've put behind you, but might not have completely released. Allow Inanna to empty your backpack and lighten your load, so you can rise and be reborn anew.

Build Your Altar

Colors Deep red, black, deep purple

Numerology 4 – Even bridges need firm foundations

Tarot Card Death – The ability to transform, transmute, and transcend

Gemstones Topaz, smoky quartz, obsidian, jet, onyx

Plant Remedy Manzanita – Being open to transforming cycles

Fragrance Sandalwood – Awakens your sensuality

Scorpio Victories and Challenges

Say all of the statements in this section out loud. Then, underline the phrase that means the most to you. Use the phrase as your special affirmation for manifesting throughout this phase of the moon.

"When the student needs to learn, the teacher appears." Today, I recognize that the Law of Reflection is in operation. I have become aware of this through my over-indulgence of judgment and criticism of other people. I am aware that when my judgment is running rampant, I am in need of a teacher who can interpret this judgment as reflection, so I can see my judgments as my teachers and use them to re-interpret myself. I seek counsel with someone who has the ability to listen to me, hear me, and give me the space I need to see myself. I have become confused by spending too much time looking outside of myself for the answers. Perhaps my authority systems, like my religion or my family traditions, no longer serve me and I need to use this confusion to become aware of a new, more self-reliant way to live my life.

The Law of Reflection

Whatever I judge is what I am, what I fear, or what I lack. I make a list of my judgments:

I rewrite each judgment in the form of a question:
Am I _____? Do I fear _____? Do I lack _____?

Example 1: I judge Mary's wealth. Do I fear wealth? Do I lack wealth? Am I wealthy in my own way and forgetting to acknowledge my own ability to manifest?

Example 2: I judge John's "be perfect" attitude. Do I fear perfection? Do I lack perfection? Have I forgotten to recognize my own perfection?

In moving through this process, I reconnect to myself and find my own authority today. I send blessings to others whose reflection has so beautifully shown me myself today. I now know and cherish my judgments as my greatest teachers and set myself free today.

Scorpio Homework

Scorpios manifest best by being a private investigator, detective, probate attorney, mystery writer, mythologist, Tarot reader, symbolist, hospice worker, transition counselor, mortician, sex surrogate, or in forensic medicine.

The Scorpio moon cycle asks you to transform. In order to do this you must transmute sex drive into creativity, physical comfort into serving the greater good, money into higher value, fear into light, animosity into understanding, ambition into service to beauty, pride into humility, separation into unity, control into harmony, and power into empowerment.

Manifesting List

This or something better than this comes to me in an easy and pleasurable way, for the good of all concerned. Thank you, Universe!

Scorpio Manifesting Ideas

Now is the time to focus on manifesting transformation on all levels, bringing light to the dark, knowing and living cycles, knowing trust as an option, accepting change, accepting my sexuality, knowing sex is natural, knowing sex as good, and knowing sex as creative.

Gratitude List

Keep this list active throughout the moon cycle. This will bring you to a level of completion so that a new cycle of opportunity can occur in your life. Be prepared for miracles!

Sky Power Yoga

Seated Cat/Cow

You need one chair for the prop.

With your back straight sit one hand-width from the back of the chair with your feet on the floor hip-width apart. If your feet require more solid contact with the floor, place pillows or folded towels under your feet.

Sit comfortably with a straight back and gently cup knees. Breathe in and out slowly and deeply several times through your nose with your awareness on your reproductive organs.

Inhale and allow your belly to drop down as your pelvis tilts back into a subtle back bend.

As you inhale, say or think to yourself the mantra *I Transform.*

Exhale slowly as you tilt your pelvis forward and round your back slightly into a gentle forward bend while gazing down. Repeat with a smooth, continuous movement as many times as desired.

New Moon in Scorpio

How to Use the Moon Book With Your Chart

Fill in the blanks on the Cosmic Check-In page. Then look up the degree of the Moon on the chart below. Take note of the "I" statement on the outside of the wheel where the Moon is located. Now, locate the same degree on your own chart and make a note of the house and corresponding

"I" statement. Go back to the Cosmic Check-In page and circle the two statements from the charts and read what you wrote. This will give you an idea about what to expect from this moon phase on a personal level.

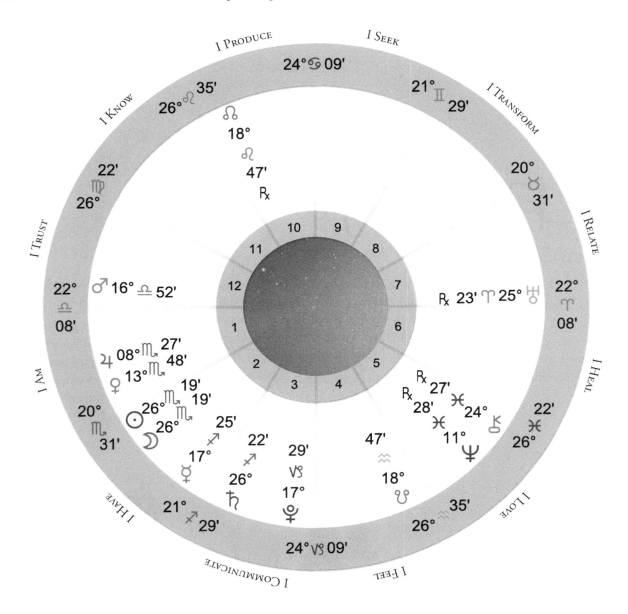

♈	Aries	♋	Cancer	♐	Sagittarius	☽	Moon	♄	Saturn	☊	North Node	V/C Void-of-Course
♉	Taurus	♌	Leo	♑	Capricorn	☿	Mercury	♅	Uranus	☋	South Node	▲ Super-Sensitivity
♊	Gemini	♍	Virgo	♒	Aquarius	♀	Venus	♆	Neptune	➡	Enters	▼ Low-Vitality
		♎	Libra	♓	Pisces	♂	Mars	♇	Pluto	℞	Retrograde	
		♏	Scorpio	☉	Sun	♃	Jupiter	⚷	Chiron	S/D	Stationary Direct	

Cosmic Check-in

Take a moment to write a brief phrase for each "I" statement. This activates all areas of your life for this creative cycle.

♏ I Transform

♐ I Seek

♑ I Produce

♒ I Know

♓ I Trust

♈ I Am

♉ I Have

♊ I Communicate

♋ I Feel

♌ I Love

♍ I Heal

♎ I Relate

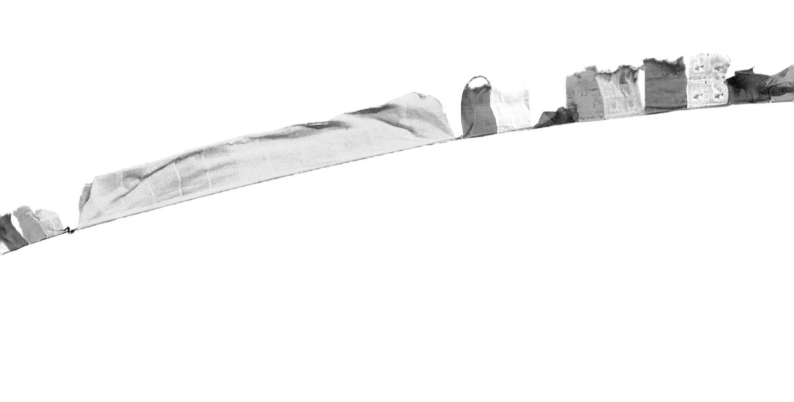

December

Planetary Highlights

Until December 4: Chiron retrograde in Pisces

Celebrate living in the moment so that pain no longer defines you.

Until 2018: Uranus retrograde in Aries

Revamp your identity. Breathe in a new flair for life. Go shopping for a new look. Ground your new inner identity from the outside in with some new shoes to kick off the next steps in your life!

Until 2018: Mars in Libra opposite Uranus in Aries

Advance your concept of self-reliance within relationships. The I of Aries is living in the we of Libra. The future paradigm is non-dual relationships where wholeness is emphasized.

December 1: Venus enters Sagittarius

It's the perfect time to celebrate with music, singing, dancing, and decorating!

December 2-3: Super Sensitivity

Love is the answer during the many days affected by the super sensitive fixed star this month. The moon transits and the planets, Saturn and Venus, gather here as well. This chaotic region in the sky is a gateway to other worlds. When the moon transits, emotions are exaggerated. When Saturn hits, karma look us right in the eye and presents us with a now or never approach. When Venus hits, all hell breaks out to test our love and what we value related to what transpired in our lives in 2017.

December 2-22: Mercury retrograde in Sagittarius

Go holiday shopping early so your holiday spirit doesn't vanish. Keep it simple with family to prevent misinterpretations. Consider breaking traditions and create a new kind of celebration.

December 3-5: Mercury and Saturn coupled in Sagittarius

Your genius mind births a major invention and your projects manifest new levels of precise intelligence.

December 4-5: Low Vitality

The moon hits the fixed star that rules low vitality and Mercury is retrograde, so we must take extra care to avoid physical and mental exhaustion.

December 7-25: Super Sensitivity

Love is the answer during the many days affected by the super sensitive fixed star this month. The moon transits and the planets, Saturn and Venus, gather here as well. This chaotic region in the sky is a gateway to other worlds. When the moon transits, emotions are exaggerated. When Saturn hits, karma look us right in the eye and presents us with a now or never approach. When Venus hits, all hell breaks out to test our love and what we value related to what transpired in our lives in 2017.

December 9: Mars enters Scorpio

Lookout! On everyone's agenda: transforming creativity, power, pleasure zones.

December 17-21: Sun, Moon, and Saturn tripled in Sagittarius

The universe asks us for a report card. What did you accomplish with your potential, your inner awareness, and the wisdom gifted to you during 2017?

December 19: Saturn enters Capricorn

Best news of the year—expect great things to happen, and they will! Transformational leadership returns. Capricorns, let Saturn guide you to a new way of being.

December 21: Winter Solstice—Sun enters Capricorn

Celebrate the earth's birthday! The longest night of the year takes us into dreamtime so we can birth ourselves anew in spring.

December 24: Venus enters Capricorn

A sudden urge to be practical tickles your fancy.

Sunday	Monday	Tuesday	Wednesday	Thursday	Friday	Saturday
					1 ⚷♅℞ ☽V/C 5:53PM ♀→♐ 1:15 AM 8. Abundance knows no limits.	**2** ⚷♅☿℞ ▲ ☽→♊ 1:20 PM ☿ S/℞ 29°♐18' 11:35 PM 9. Embrace the joy of the moment.
3 ⚷♅☿℞ ▲ ○ 11°♊40' 7:47AM 10. See the holidays in a new way.	**4** ⚷♅☿℞ ▼ ☽V/C 11:12 AM ☽→♋ 12:36 PM ⚷ S/D 24°♓19' 1:47AM 11. Bring all the loose ends together.	**5** ♅☿℞ ▼ 3. Set aside some time for play today.	**6** ♅☿℞ ☽V/C 9:55 AM ☽→♌ 12:37PM 4. Make your plans simple and clear.	**7** ♅☿℞ ▲ 5. Be flexible and change readily.	**8** ♅☿℞ ▲ ☽V/C 2:40 PM ☽→♍ 3:08PM 6. Decorate with things you love.	**9** ♅☿℞ ▲ ♂→♏ 1:00AM 7. Where can your brilliance shine?
10 ♅☿℞ ▲ ☽V/C 7:02 PM ☽→♎ 9:00PM 8. When shopping, shop wisely.	**11** ♅☿℞ ▲ 9. Go to hear a holiday concert.	**12** ♅☿℞ ▲ Hanukkah 10. Update your holiday décor.	**13** ♅☿℞ ▲ ☽V/C 4:26 AM ☽→♏ 5:58 AM 11. Rely on the assistance of others.	**14** ♅☿℞ ▲ ☽V/C 5:42 PM 3. If it isn't fun, why do it?	**15** ♅☿℞ ▲ ☽→♐ 5:07 PM 4. Build from the bottom up.	**16** ♅☿℞ ▲ 5. Be comfortable with spontaneity.
17 ♅☿℞ ▲ ● 26°♐31' 10:30PM 6. Add new friends to your party list.	**18** ♅☿℞ ▲ ☽V/C 5:09 AM ☽→♑ 5:33 AM 7. Read a recommended book.	**19** ♅☿℞ ▲ ♄→♑ 8:49 PM 8. Be sure a sale item is worth it.	**20** ♅☿℞ ▲ ☽V/C 7:36 AM ☽→♒ 6:29 PM 9. Enjoy the essence of the season.	**21** ♅☿℞ ▲ Winter Solstice ☉→♑ 8:29AM 10. Honor what good you have done.	**22** ♅℞ ☿ S/D 13°♐01 5:52PM 11. Celebrate things coming together.	**23** ♅℞ ▲ ☽V/C 2:12 AM ☽→♓ 6:41 AM 3. Find humor in life.
24 ♅℞ ▲ ☽V/C 6:47 PM ♀→♑ 9:27PM 4. Too much stuckness ruins fun.	**25** ♅℞ ▲ Christmas Day ☽→♈ 4:26 PM 5. When making plans, stay flexible.	**26** ♅℞ 6. Happily do someone a favor.	**27** ♅℞ ☽V/C 12:57 PM ☽→♉ 10:23 PM 7. Do research for charitible giving.	**28** ♅℞ 8. We become prosperous by giving.	**29** ♅℞ ☽V/C 6:00 AM 9. Celebrate joyfully.	**30** ♅℞ ☽→♊ 12:30 AM 10. See the year ahead as a new start.
31 ♅℞ New Year's Eve ☽V/C 3:38 PM 11. Rejoice in the journey of life.	January 1, 2018 ☽→♋ 12:10 AM					

♈ Aries	♎ Libra	☉ Sun	♄ Saturn	☊ North Node	▲ Super Sensitivity	6. Love
♉ Taurus	♏ Scorpio	☽ Moon	♅ Uranus	☋ South Node	▼ Low Vitality	7. Learning
♊ Gemini	♐ Sagittarius	☿ Mercury	♆ Neptune	➡ Enters	2. Balance	8. Money
♋ Cancer	♑ Capricorn	♀ Venus	♇ Pluto	℞ Retrograde	3. Fun	9. Spirituality
♌ Leo	♒ Aquarius	♂ Mars	⚷ Chiron	S/D Stationary Direct	4. Structure	10. Visionary
♍ Virgo	♓ Pisces	♃ Jupiter		V/C Void-of-Course	5. Action	11. Completion

Full Moon in Gemini

December 3rd, 7:47 AM

Statement I Communicate
Body Lungs and Hands
Mind Academic
Spirit Intelligence
Element Air – Brings change and promotes curiosity, insight, and concepts.

Degree Choice Points
  11° Gemini 40'
Light Assertiveness
Shadow Demanding
Wisdom Use mantra to experience sound and time in a new way.

Sixth House Moon
  4° Gemini 40'
Sixth House Umbrella Theme
  I Heal /I Communicate – The way you manage your body and appearance.
Light The Wise Sage
Shadow The Know-It-All
Wisdom Accept assistance from family and friends.

Karmic Awakening

Karma is activated when there is a conflict between knowing and loving. If the expression of love inspires knowing, then all will be well. If your love is solid within yourself, then peer or group pressure will not challenge it.

The Sun is Opposite the Moon

Full moons are always in opposition to the Sun. This creates a feeling of tension between where you want to shine and how your feelings are flowing on a sensory level about the Sun's directive. The two forces seem like they are working against each other, yet they are on the same team displaying different techniques to obtain the same mission. The Gemini/Sagittarius polarity creates tension between community ideas and global thinking.

Gemini Goddess

Saraswati beckons you to withdraw from the party scene and into the quiet, contemplative process to dream your finest creations into being. Goddess of all creative endeavors: writing, art, dance, and music, Saraswati can assist you in your waking hours and in the dreamtime.

Get out your crayons, markers, paints, and pastels, and create a massive mind map with your happiness and fulfillment at the core (your new seedpod). What sprouts from the center? What branches off? Trust the process to generate ideas to rebirth you into joyful action! Post the map where you will see it often so it can serve as an active reminder of who you are and where you're headed!

Build Your Altar

Colors Bright yellow, orange, multi-colors
Numerology 10 – See the holidays in a new way
Tarot Card Lovers – Connecting to wholeness
Gemstones Yellow diamond, citrine, yellow jade, yellow topaz
Plant remedy Morning Glory – Thinking with your heart, not your head
Fragrance Iris – The ability to focus the mind

Clearing the Slate

Sixty hours before the full moon negative traits connected to the astro-sign might become activated to trigger what needs to be released during the full moon phase. You may notice that you are not listening to others and overriding what others are saying by talking too much. Watch out for gossiping or omitting the truth. Make a list of the triggers and do Ho'oponopono, a Hawaiian Huna ritual for forgiveness. Look in the mirror, and for each negative trait, tell yourself *I am sorry, I forgive you, thank you for your awareness,* and *I love you.*

Gemini Victories and Challenges

Say all of the statements in this section out loud. Then, underline the phrase that means the most to you. Use the phrase as your special affirmation for recalibrating throughout this phase of the moon.

Today, I blend my old self with my new self, my physical reality with my spiritual awareness, my positive thoughts with my negative thoughts, my past with my present, my feminine with my masculine, my rewards with my losses, my ups with my downs, and my higher self with my lower self. It is a day for me to refine and fine tune my life by looking at my extremes. I recognize what inspires me and what keeps me stuck. I find my center today by acknowledging my extremes. I am aware that balance comes to those who are able to locate the space in the center of these opposite energy fields.

When I am in my center, my polarities are in motion. Healing cannot occur unless my polarities are moving and I know that healing is motion. I am ready for a healing today. I know that by visiting my opposites, and determining their vast opposition to each other, I can find the paradoxes that I have chosen for myself and begin to heal. I am willing to experiment with this blending of opposites and become the alchemist of my own life. When I blend all aspects of myself, rather than separating them, I can truly become whole. Today is a day to integrate, rather than separate, in order to release the spark of light that stays prisoner when my polarities are in operation. When I find balance, motion occurs and the Law of Harmony takes over, putting paradoxical energies to rest, thus breaking the crystallization of polarity. The Law of Harmony is beauty in motion and promotes the flow of color, light, sound, and movement into form. Balance is a condition that keeps my spark in motion. I become the vertical line in the center of polarity today and carry the secret of balance. Balance cannot be my goal; motion is my goal today. When I am in motion, I can take action to evolve and to express all of myself freely.

Gemini Homework

Sit still and invite silence into your space. Stay quiet and still for at least 5 minutes. During this time take an inventory and see where you have interrupted people in the middle of their sentences. Now is the time to make a conscious effort to allow others the space to express their thoughts. Keep sitting in silence and feel the frustration, while embracing the power of silence.

Recalibrating List

Say this statement out loud three times before writing your recalibrating list:

I am a free spiritual being and it is my desire to be free to think and to express myself fully.

From this day forward I resolve to be true — first to myself and my highest self, and then to the highest self in me which is the Source of Love That I Am.

Gemini Recalibrating Ideas

Now is the time to activate a game change in my life, and give up my attitude about unfinished business, shallow communication, old files and office clutter, broken communication devices, lies I tell myself, temptation to gossip, restlessness, over-thinking, and vacillation.

Activate Acceleration

By acknowledging what you have recalibrated and overcome, you activate your acceleration. Keep this list active during this moon cycle.

Sky Power Yoga

Reclined Heart Opener

You need two bath towels and one to two pillows for the prop.

Fold two towels in half lengthwise, roll them into a log, and place them on the floor. Put both pillows on top of the rolled towels to support your back, neck, and head in the pose.

Sit on the floor with the support prop behind you.

Lean back onto your elbows and then lower your back onto your support prop. This creates a gentle opening across your chest. If you find your head dangling over the top edge, shift your prop towards your head to support your head and neck fully.

Place your arms out at a 45-degree angle with palms facing upward at your sides.

Relax. Close your eyes. Breathe in and out slowly and deeply several times through your nose keeping your awareness on your lungs and hands.

Inhale and keep your awareness on the expansion of your lungs. Exhale softly and slowly as you say or think to yourself the mantra *I Communicate*. Relax fully into the support prop and the pose. Enjoy breathing with the mantra for a few minutes.

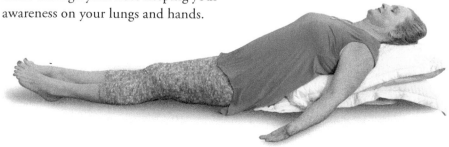

Full Moon in Gemini

How to Use the Moon Book With Your Chart

Fill in the blanks on the Cosmic Check-In page. Then look up the degree of the Moon on the chart below. Take note of the "I" statement on the outside of the wheel where the Moon is located. Now, locate the same degree on your own chart and make a note of the house and corresponding

"I" statement. Go back to the Cosmic Check-In page and circle the two statements from the charts and read what you wrote. This will give you an idea about what to expect from this moon phase on a personal level.

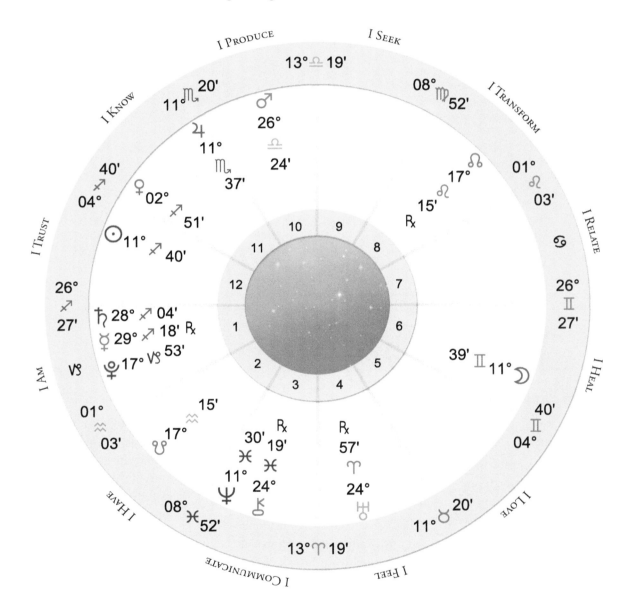

♈	Aries	♋	Cancer	♐	Sagittarius	☽	Moon	♄	Saturn	☊	North Node	V/C Void-of-Course
♉	Taurus	♌	Leo	♑	Capricorn	☿	Mercury	♅	Uranus	☋	South Node	▲ Super-Sensitivity
♊	Gemini	♍	Virgo	♒	Aquarius	♀	Venus	♆	Neptune	➡	Enters	▼ Low-Vitality
		♎	Libra	♓	Pisces	♂	Mars	♇	Pluto	℞	Retrograde	
		♏	Scorpio	☉	Sun	♃	Jupiter	⚷	Chiron	S/D	Stationary Direct	

Cosmic Check-in

Take a moment to write a brief phrase for each "I" statement. This activates all areas of your life for this creative cycle.

♊ I Communicate

♋ I Feel

♌ I Love

♍ I Heal

♎ I Relate

♏ I Transform

♐ I Seek

♑ I Produce

♒ I Know

♓ I Trust

♈ I Am

♉ I Have

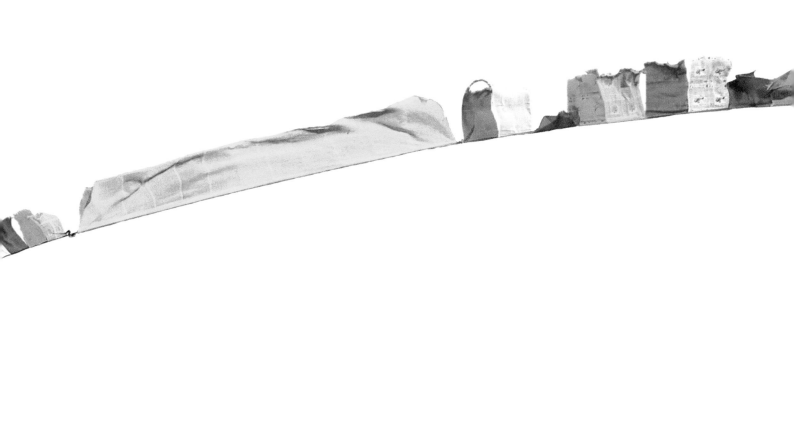

New Moon in Sagittarius

December 17th, 10:30 PM

Statement I Seek
Body Thighs
Mind Philosophical
Spirit Inspiration
Element Fire – Inspiring, leadership, charisma, igniting, and adventurous.

Degree Choice Points
26° Sagittarius 31'

Light Profound Relationships
Shadow Subjection
Wisdom Use the abstract to create a new vision.

Fourth House Moon
9° Sagittarius 6'

Fourth House Umbrella Theme
I Feel/I Seek – How your early environmental training was, how that set your foundation for living, and why you chose your mother.

Light Promoting and Publishing
Shadow Biased Vision
Wisdom Separation anxiety results from a detachment—either positive or negative.

When the Sun is in Sagittarius

Now is the time for greater expansion of consciousness. Sagittarius is about exterminating all of the man-eating symbols of our illusions, harmful thoughts, inertia, prejudices, and superstitions that hide behind our excuses. It is truth time, so that the Soul Goal of the Sagittarius can come into being and direct its light toward greater aspiration. Questions to ask yourself at this time are: What is my goal for myself? What is my goal for my nation? What is my goal for humanity? All goals get stimulated during this time.

Sagittarius Goddess

Let Persephone, who chose to stay in the Underworld half of the year and became the Queen of Death, be your guide as you enter the dark time of the year. Harvest is over and you now allow the land to become fallow – plowed, but unseeded. Persephone, in the version of the myth unspoiled by patriarchy, hears the cries of those stuck in purgatory, and is moved to voluntarily guide the anguished toward the completion of their spiritual journeys.

Of Persephone, also known as the maiden Kore, Plato wrote, "She is wise and touches that which is in motion." Where might you be stuck and how can Persephone get you moving in the right direction? What in your life do you seek to transform? Who do you wish to become?

Build Your Altar

Colors Deep purple, deep blue, turquoise
Numerology 6 – Add new friends to your party list
Tarot Card Temperance – Blending physical and spiritual
Gemstones Turquoise, lapis
Plant Remedy Madia – Seeing the target and hitting it
Fragrance Magnolia – Expanded beauty

Sagittarius Victories *and* Challenges

Say all of the statements in this section out loud. Then, underline the phrase that means the most to you. Use the phrase as your special affirmation for manifesting throughout this phase of the moon.

Destiny is in my favor today. I know, without a doubt, that I cannot make a wrong turn today. I access my blueprint to ensure perfect timing for all opportunities to be open to me today. I promise to be open to these opportunities, knowing full well that today is my day. I am on time and in time today. My destiny is here and working in my favor. I see all that is available to me today and claim my pathway to success. I pay attention to what comes my way today and know that it is an opening for good fortune to be my reality. I am ready to accept my good fortune now. All I have to do is move in the direction of my truth. I know that my truth is my good fortune. I trust in coincidence and synchronicity to provide me with direction to my destiny. All points of action lead me to my true expression. I can see clearly into my future today with great optimism. I intend it. I allow it. So be it. All is in Divine Order.

Mantra during this Time (*repeat this 10 times out loud*)

"My truth is my good fortune. My timing is perfect. I trust that all that comes to me today is in my highest and best good. I am open to optimism. The drum of destiny beats in my favor. So be it!"

Sagittarius Homework

Sagittarians manifest best through teaching, publishing and writing, travel, spiritual adventures, and as tour group leaders, airline and cruise ship personnel, evangelical ministers, philosophers, anthropologists, linguists, and translators.

The Sagittarius moon cycle creates a magnetic matrix that stimulates us to take direction towards becoming one with a goal and then sheds light on the path. In the ancient mystery schools, Sagittarius moons were used to set the stage for candidates to reach higher levels of awareness by inspiring their desire to reach a goal and then to step toward the goal. It is time now to become one with your goal.

Manifesting List

This or something better than this comes to me in an easy and pleasurable way, for the good of all concerned. Thank you, Universe!

Sagittarius Manifesting Ideas

Now is the time to focus on manifesting truth, teaching and study, understanding advanced ideas, optimism and inspiration, bliss, goals, travel and adventure, and philosophy and culture.

Gratitude List

Keep this list active throughout the moon cycle. This will bring you to a level of completion so that a new cycle of opportunity can occur in your life. Be prepared for miracles!

Sky Power Yoga

Reclined Windshield Wipers

No prop is needed.

Lay on the floor face up with your legs bent and feet on the floor hip-width apart. Place arms out at your sides with palms facing down.

Relax. Close your eyes. Breathe in and out slowly and deeply several times through your nose with your awareness on your thighs. To create the windshield wipers movement, rock both your knees to the left and then to the right. Connect the movement with your breath—inhale and move knees to the left and exhale moving knees to the right

Inhale softly as you say or think to yourself the mantra *I Seek* and move your legs to the left.

Exhale softly and move legs right. Repeat as desired.

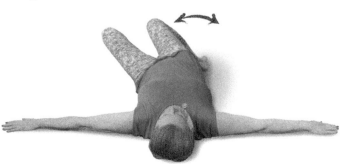

New Moon in Sagittarius

How to Use the Moon Book With Your Chart

Fill in the blanks on the Cosmic Check-In page. Then look up the degree of the Moon on the chart below. Take note of the "I" statement on the outside of the wheel where the Moon is located. Now, locate the same degree on your own chart and make a note of the house and corresponding

"I" statement. Go back to the Cosmic Check-In page and circle the two statements from the charts and read what you wrote. This will give you an idea about what to expect from this moon phase on a personal level.

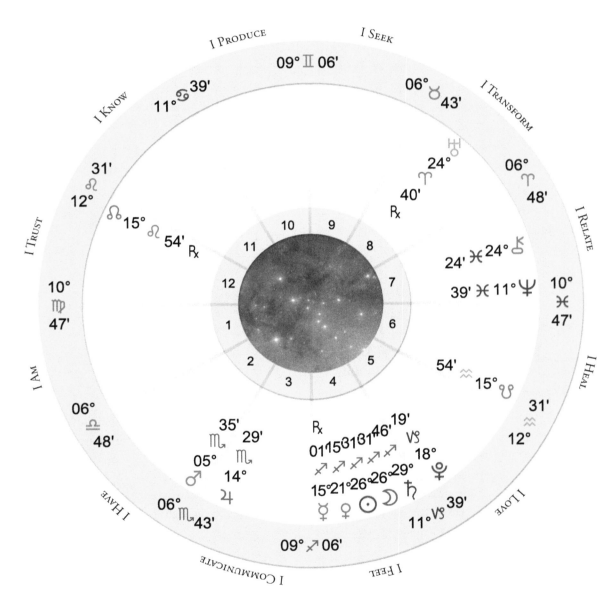

♈	Aries	♋	Cancer	♐	Sagittarius	☽	Moon	♄ Saturn
♉	Taurus	♌	Leo	♑	Capricorn	☿	Mercury	♅ Uranus
♊	Gemini	♍	Virgo	♒	Aquarius	♀	Venus	♆ Neptune
		♎	Libra	♓	Pisces	♂	Mars	♇ Pluto
		♏	Scorpio	☉	Sun	♃	Jupiter	⚷ Chiron

☊	North Node
☋	South Node
➔	Enters
℞	Retrograde
S/D	Stationary Direct

V/C Void-of-Course
▲ Super-Sensitivity
▼ Low-Vitality

Cosmic Check-in

Take a moment to write a brief phrase for each "I" statement. This activates all areas of your life for this creative cycle.

⚐ I Seek

♑ I Produce

♒ I Know

♓ I Trust

♈ I Am

♉ I Have

♊ I Communicate

♋ I Feel

♌ I Love

♍ I Heal

♎ I Relate

♏ I Transform

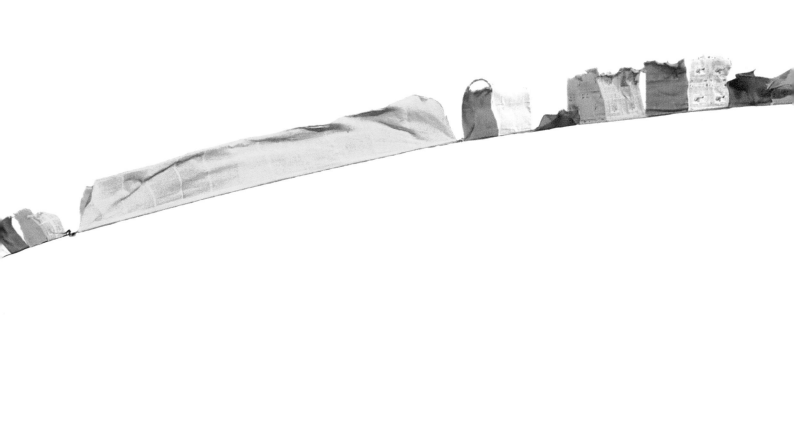

About the Author

Beatrex Quntanna

Tarot expert, published author, symbolist, poet, lecturer—Beatrex is one of the luminaries of our time. Synthesizing more than 40 years of spiritual teachings, intuitive skills, and conventional counseling, she translates this wealth of wisdom into practical language making it accessible to all and applicable in today's world. Known for being "the teacher's teacher," her experience and advice has served as an invaluable support for many of today's spiritual teachers and professional psychics. She guides with profound insight, compassion for the human experience, and humor; inspiring personal growth and activating an inner-knowing in her students that sparks a self-confidence to walk tall in this world as a spiritual being.

Her life's work is showing how to Live Love Every Day by *living* astrology, not just intellectualizing it—teaching others how to ebb and flow with the natural cycles of the Moon and the cosmos, rather than working against them. She teaches this through Moon Classes held regularly throughout the year, and is the creator of *Living by the Light of the Moon*, a popular annual workbook that takes you step-by-step through her process.

Beatrex has written the ultimate book on the Tarot and its symbols, *Tarot: A Universal Language*, which has been reviewed by magazines in Europe as well as in the United States. She is the creator and co-presenter of the popular Annual Tarot Workshop with Michael Makay, designed as a complete support system to enhance your understanding of how best to work with the transformative energies of the upcoming year.

Beatrex's many print credits, as well as numerous radio, TV, and video appearances include:

- Regular guest blogger for Satiama.com and True Nature Healing Arts
- Contributing author to two anthologies by Maria Yracébûrû – *Prophetic Voices* and *Ah-Kine Remembrance*
- Monthly guest on *Spirit Seeker Hour* with host Cynde Meyer – tune in to *Spirit Seeker Magazine's* internet radio show on the first Tuesday of each month to get a free psychic mini-reading
- *Cosmic Check-In with Beatrex Quntanna* – a monthly YouTube show produced by Boyd Martin

Beatrex teaches ongoing astrology classes, facilitates a regular meditation group, and continues to be available for private group workshops in Encinitas, California.

Interested in ongoing Moon Classes and workshops with Beatrex?
Contact her at beatrex@cox.net or visit www.beatrex.com

For Moon-related products created by Beatrex, visit
www.MyMoonBook.com

Other works by Beatrex

2017 The Year of Acceleration Wall Calendar

Created by Beatrex Quntanna and Michael Makay with art and design by Jennifer Masters

2017 advances you to new heights of awareness and accelerates your knowledge beyond what you imagined possible.

The dance of the Uranus and Jupiter opposition throughout the entire year will accelerate you beyond current paradigms. These two planets have huge expansive fields as their spheres of influence. Make their vastness your friend in 2017; Jupiter will bring good fortune and Uranus will take you to unexplored places. Embrace and move beyond each of their polarities so that neither separation nor contraction can occur. The expansion provided by both planets is unconventional, and will create the ideal acceleration to evolve your life beyond what you have imagined is possible for yourself.

Our 2017 calendar gives you insight into:

- **Astrological Highlights** that are easy to integrate into your life
- **Daily Intentions** based on Tibetan numerology by Michael Makay
- **Monthly Planetary Retrogrades** to keep you on track
- **Super-Sensitivity** and **Low-Vitality** days to prevent burnout and exhaustion
- **New, Full, and Void Moons** by time, astro-sign, and degree and the Sun's movement through the zodiac calculated by Katherine Sale

"*The Moon Book Calendar* has become an indispensable tool in my spiritual journey. Simple and easy to use, the calendar has helped me to understand and work with the cycles of the Sun, Moon and Stars to live a life of greater joy."

— Robin Simmons

"I consult *The Moon Book Calendar* to know when to make decisions, when to back up my computer, when to go to bed and rest, when to schedule classes, when it's good to begin projects, or travel. I use it to stay sane when I'm feeling low energy and see from the calendar that it's not just me! I have two calendars—one at home and one at work because the information is that important!"

— Kaliani Cynthia Hupper

To order, call 1-760-944-6020 or go to www.MyMoonBook.com

Tarot: A Universal Language

By Beatrex Quntanna

Experiencing the Road of Life Through Symbols

Embark on this fascinating journey through the unfolding Story of Life as told by the Universal Language of the Tarot. This book contains innovative avenues to understand the tarot through the author's in-depth knowledge of symbology.

Learn how to quickly read and interpret the Tarot by following this simple, informative, and illustrated guide. Use the expanded symbology section to understand each symbol depicted on the Minor and Major Arcana cards.

This book includes an interpretation of all 78 Tarot cards, plus readings created by this nationally-known Tarot teacher, reader, and symbolist.

To order, call 1-760-944-6020 or go to www.beatrex.com

"Brilliantly Engineered."   *"Amazingly Accurate."*   *"A refreshing, uncluttered approach to learning the Tarot."*

"Her exceptional background in symbology and numerology, as well as her extraordinary psychic insight, make this book unique among Tarot books, and a must-have reference for the Tarot novice and professional alike."

The Tarot Online Course

With Beatrex Quntanna

Experience the amazing interpretation and wisdom behind each and every Tarot card from Beatrex. It will now be available online for the first time ever. Beatrex has over forty years experience giving Tarot readings and teaching the Tarot to her students.

Now this wealth of knowledge is available to you to study at your leisure...

- High-quality instructional videos
- Study aids
- Fun quizzes
- Insightful activities

Whether you are on a journey to learn the Tarot for your own enlightenment or whether you want to do Tarot card readings for others, this is the course for you. Beatrex fills the course with her insightful wisdom, funny stories, and deep, anchored knowledge of the Tarot. Don't miss this course.

For more information, go to www.MyMoonBook.com

CPSIA information can be obtained
at www.ICGtesting.com
Printed in the USA
BVOW07s2311020517
482977BV00006B/116/P